THE COMPLETE BOOK OF THE GNOME

ALL YOU'LL EVER NEED OR WANT TO KNOW

THE COMPLETE BOOK OF THE GNOME

ALL YOU'LL EVER NEED OR WANT TO KNOW

MARTIN CORNWALL

Produced by AA Publishing

Published by AA Publishing, a trading name of Automobile Association Developments Limited, whose registered office is Norfolk House, Priestley Road, Basingstoke, Hampshire RG24 9NY; registered number 1878835.

Find out more about AA Publishing from our Web site at www.theaa.co.uk.

ISBN 0 7495 0709 8

A CIP catalogue record for this book is available from the British Library.

Author: Martin Cornwall

Model maker: John Plowman

Studio photography: Contrast Photography Ltd, Basingstoke; Paul Forrester, Britannia Studios, London

Picture researcher: Kathy Lockley

Colour separation by Fotographics Ltd

Printed and bound in Italy by Stige, Turin

Contents

AN INTRODUCTION TO NANOLOGY

THE TERM IS DERIVED FROM THE GREEK WORD 'NANOS' – DWARF. Powerful and contradictory emotions are aroused by garden gnomes. Born in aristocratic circles in the great days of Victorian England, and brought up in style in titled rockeries, they fell foul of the gardening writers who have dominated 20th-century taste and slipped down the social ladder, banished to disregarded suburbs and the neatly kept gardens of bungalows as victims of the English class system.

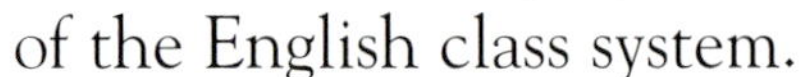

LEFT
The archetypal garden gnome of today, busy looking after the garden of his proud owner

ABOVE
Many gnomes are shy and retiring creatures, preferring to hide in the depths of the garden

Owners of gnomes love them dearly. Some value them as symbols and representatives of the harmony of nature, others as luck-bringers or substitutes for children or pets, and they are the centre of much affectionate humour. Their detractors, on the other hand, view them with pained and supercilious contempt as appalling, sentimental kitsch.

Loved or loathed, cherished or condemned, desired or derided, garden gnomes are a legacy of the ancient human need to populate the whole world with spirits, their presence sensed in trees and boulders, caves and streams. These spirits account for odd, inexplicable happenings and unaccountable noises, for animals panicking for no discernible cause, for objects strangely going missing and, equally surprisingly, turning up again, for echoes in the mountains and mysterious sounds in mines. A persistent, anxious theme of stories about them is their liking for stealing a human baby and leaving one of their own in its place as a changeling, much like a cuckoo in the nest.

DARK AND LIGHT, GOOD AND EVIL

These beings are generally diminutive in size, human-like in many ways, but credited with eerie and magical powers. Some of them live close to human beings in houses and farm buildings, some are found in fields and woods, and others inhabit mountains and the remote depths of forests.They are often kindly disposed to mankind, but some are malevolent and dangerous, while many of them are not exactly either good or evil, but uncanny and unchancy. You can never be quite sure of them and they are never safely offended. These are not the pretty little gauzy-winged fairies of Victorian fancy, but earthier and more formidable creatures. It is wiser not to call them by their real names, but to employ polite terms such as 'little people', 'gentle people', 'hidden people' or 'good fellows'. In the Isle of Man they were referred to cautiously as 'themselves' or 'they'.

In 1831 when a Scottish workman found the Lewis chessmen – a set of 84 superb carved chess pieces – inside a cave near Uig on the Isle of Lewis, he took to his heels and ran for his life, convinced he had stumbled on a group of the 'wee folk', fast asleep. His wife persuaded him to go back and bring them out, and most of them are now in the British Museum.

PREHISTORIC BEINGS

All sorts of speculative theories have been advanced about the origins of the dwarfs. The idea that they were originally a real pigmy race of enslaved mineworkers, forced to delve and toil in prehistoric pits and caverns, has few serious supporters. The suggestion that a race of itinerant specialist miners worked in Central Europe in early times is aired occasionally, but there is no convincing evidence for it. A more persuasive idea, first suggested in the 1890s by Scottish folklorist David MacRitchie, is that folk traditions contain distant memories of an older, more primitive people, dark and diminutive, driven away into the mountains, forests and fens by their more advanced successors, who regarded them with an uneasy blend of curiosity, respect and mistrust. Stone-Age flint arrowheads were later called 'elf-shot' in England and Scotland.

There are dwarfish gods and supernatural beings in many traditions. Ancient Egyptian texts, for instance, mention dwarf gods who are often aspects of the sun-god Re, or of the sky-god Horus as a child, and are considered helpful and protective.

The popular protective god Bes was represented as a pot-bellied, bandy-legged dwarf in a leopard skin with an ostrich feather stuck in his hair, poking his tongue out as a rude, repelling gesture to the evil spirits he kept at bay. His image was often carved on bedposts.

The Greeks in classical times had a craftsman-god named Hephaestus, the divine smith, who was probably originally connected with the fire of erupting volcanoes. The Romans called him Vulcan. Lame and stunted, ugly and uncouth, with the brawny arms of a smith, he possessed the magical powers with which the first smiths were credited in the Bronze Age, and the dwarfs of European lore were skilled smiths. Other theorists have pointed to the Dactyls, or literally 'fingers', who, according to Greek mythology, lived on Mount Ida in Crete, had magical powers and invented the smith's craft: though whether they were called 'fingers' because they were small or because they were supremely skilled with their hands is uncertain.

ABOVE & RIGHT *Many garden gnomes are protrayed as throwbacks to the time when dwarfs toiled underground in mines, carrying picks and shovels, hammers and axes, their faces rough and ruddy through their labours*

CAPTURED IN STONE

Two massive stone heads on the Nemrut-Dagi mountain in Turkey, dating from the 1st century BC and representing Zeus, the king of the Greek gods, and the hero Hercules have something of a gnomish look about them after centuries of weathering, with their sunken eyes, beards and tall, conical hats. Another interesting figure is the great Persian god of light, Mithras, who became popular with soldiers all over the Roman Empire and whose cult was a serious rival to Christianity in its early days. He was born in a cave, which his temples reproduced, and dwarfs have always been closely linked with caves and underground passages.

Some representations of dwarfs show them wearing a cap with a bulbous peak looking something like Mithras's characteristic cap (the *pileus*), which also resembles the 'cap of liberty' favoured by ardent French Revolutionaries in the 18th century. They wore red liberty caps and planted 'liberty trees', the tree being surmounted by a cap which was based on the special 'Phrygian bonnet' that freed Roman slaves used to put on to mark the moment of their emancipation. This is indeed a formidable provenance for so humble a creature as the garden gnome, a much-maligned and underestimated presence to be ignored at your peril.

TOP & ABOVE
The ancient features from Nemrut-Dagi and Mithras have a gnomish look about them

OUR THANKS TO...

The author and publisher gratefully acknowledge help generously give by:the following people in the preparation of this book: Ann Atkin of the Gnome Reserve; Dr Brent Elliott, Librarian of the Royal Horticultural Society; Alan Quarterman of Gnome World; James Rylands of Sotherby's; Roy Stevens of Limmex Industries and Henry Sutherland of the New Zealand Gnome Committe. Thanks also to Günter and Jutta Griebel of the Garden Dwarf Museum, Rot am See, Germany, and to Alison Layland.

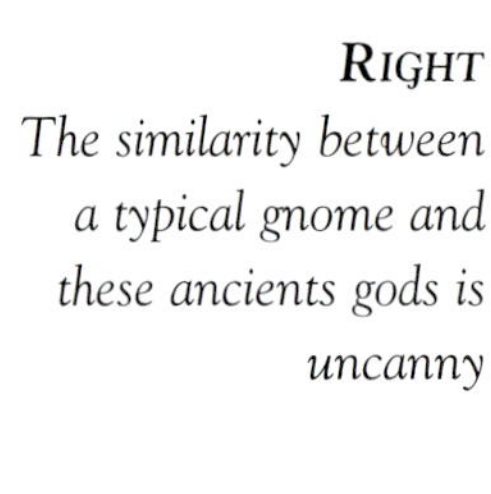

RIGHT
The similarity between a typical gnome and these ancients gods is uncanny

Ancestral Gnomes

The humble garden gnome comes of an ancient stock. The little red-capped figures which wheel their barrows or sit with their fishing rods by many a garden pond are descended from the dwarfs of Northern European mythology and folklore. They are part of the army of 'the little people' or fairy folk, whose existence was firmly believed in virtually everywhere in the world in centuries gone by: elves and pixies, *nisses* and *kobolds*, trolls, brownies, boggarts, leprechauns and many more.

FROM PAGAN BEGINNINGS

DESPITE MUCH SPECULATION and uncertainty, what is not in doubt is that today's garden gnomes hark back directly to folk traditions of the pagan peoples of Northern Europe – the Scandinavians, Germans, and Anglo-Saxons – before the coming of Christianity. Some of these traditions were written down in the 13th century by a Christian Icelander called Snorri Sturluson.

ABOVE
Icelandic bard Snorri Sturluson

A MUCH-TRAVELLED businessman and diplomat, Snorri Sturluson was a leading 'skald', or bard. In his *Prose Edda*, written as a poet's guide to imagery, he tells of two types of elves – light elves and dark elves. The light elves are fairer than the sun to look upon. They live in the sky-realm of Alfheim ('elf-home') where the sun god Frey rules, and one of the sun's names is 'glory of elves'. The dark elves, however, are black as pitch and live deep underground. The dark elves seem to be the same as the dwarfs in Sturluson's version of the Norse myth of how the world was originally the body of a colossal primeval giant, Ymir, who was killed by the gods. The mountains were made from his bones, the earth from his flesh, the sea from his blood. Dwarfs bred like maggots in the guts of his corpse and the gods gave them human form and intelligence, 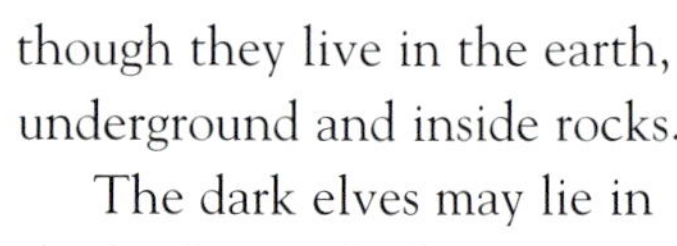though they live in the earth, underground and inside rocks.

LEFT
Gnomes often carry tools from their mining days

The dark elves may lie in the background of a story current later in Europe and Iceland, that the elves were descended from some of Eve's children by Adam – the ones she had not got round to washing when God came to see them. She hid them, but God knew and declared that what was concealed from him should be concealed from men. So the unwashed infants were banished to woods and moors and rocks, and became the ancestors of elves and country spirits – the *huldre* or *huldufolk*, 'the hidden people'.

Other Christian authors adapted this mythology by saying that God had created the dwarfs specially to mine the mountains and exploit their concealed treasures of gold, silver and precious stones, unknown to men. He made them wise and skilful, and they understood all the mysteries of their craft and knew the secret properties of gems – which could impart physical strength or make the wearer invisible.

Snorri's distinction between the light and the dark elves may well have been somewhat simplistic, perhaps reflecting what were originally two aspects of the same beings: the beautiful and good because they promoted fertility, and the dark and sinister because they were the dead and were buried in the ground.

Dwarfs, Magic & Mystery

Snorri's dwarfs were skilled craftsmen who made magic treasures for the gods. Loki, the mischievous god of fire, one day for a lark cut off the beautiful golden hair of the wife of Thor, the god of thunder. Frightened of what Thor would do to him, he found two skilled dwarf smiths who forged false hair for her out of gold so fine that it was as silky as her own and would grow on her head. They also made a magic ship for Frey and the great spear Gungnir (meaning 'swaying one') with magic runes carved on its point for the god Odin. Loki bet two other dwarf master-craftsmen that they could not match these three treasures. Piqued, they set to work and forged a gold-bristled boar, the great gold ring Draupnir ('dripper'), which multiplied itself by exuding eight more golden rings every ninth night, and the hammer named Mjollnir (possibly 'lightning'), which would hit any target at which it was aimed and then return to the thrower's hand. Loki had wagered his head, but when the time came to pay up he ingeniously and successfully argued that, although the triumphant dwarfs had won his head, the terms of the bet did not allow them to sever his neck.

Sturluson also told of Loki going to the realm of the dark elves in search of a dwarf named Andvari, who owned a fabulous hoard of treasure. Finding Andvari resting in a pool in the form of a fish, Loki forced him to give up all his gold, including a particularly precious magic ring which the dwarf tried to keep hidden. He begged to be allowed to keep the ring, because with it he would become rich again, but Loki insisted on taking it. Then the dwarf said that the ring would destroy everyone who owned it. This is one source of the epic tale of the treasure of the Nibelungs, basis for the cycle of *Ring* operas by Richard Wagner(1813–83).

Above
One of the many poems dedicated to elves and their gatherings

Above
The Norse god Thor, whose wife's hair was cut off by Loki, god of fire

LITTLE-GNOME FACT

The word for dwarf in Old Norse was *dverg* and the widespread belief that dwarfs were responsible for echoes heard among lonely mountain peaks – where they were said to have a trick of repeating the last words of any conversation they overheard – was expressed in the word for echo (*dvergmali*).

TALES OF MYTH AND LEGEND

The first pagan English peoples, or Anglo-Saxons, who had overrun most of England by AD 600, brought their beliefs in the little people with them. They knew of mountain elves and field elves, wood elves and water elves. Anglo-Saxon attitudes were matched and paralleled by the traditions of the Celtic people whom the English conquered or displaced, while the Norse settlers who afterwards occupied eastern and northern England and parts of Scotland, and established a lodgement in Ireland, carried their similar pre-Christian beliefs to their new homes.

These pagan traditions survived the coming of Christianity to the North and blended with the new religion. Gerald of Wales, a 12th-century Norman-Welsh cleric, told a story about a boy named Elidor, who was taken by two dwarfs through a dark tunnel to a beautiful underground realm of rivers, meadows and woods, rich in gold, where there was no sun, moon or stars. Treated kindly, he met the king and his courtiers, fair of

ABOVE
The troll king surveys his realm from his hideaway at Efteling in Holland

RIGHT
This mischievous pixie-like creature with the evil grin is reminiscent of a satyr

complexion with long, luxuriant hair. Their diminutive horses and dogs were proportionate to their own size and they spoke disapprovingly of human vices. The boy justified their contempt by trying to steal some of their gold. As a result, he could never find his way back to their delightful land, to his great regret.

In England in the same period, the courtier and author Walter Map reported another popular story about the dwarf king of an underground realm, the entrance to which was a cave in a high cliff. The king had a big head and a flowing red beard, rode a goat and wore the skin of a spotted fawn as a jerkin. Like the satyrs of Greek and Roman mythology, his lower parts were hairy and he had the hoofs of a goat. His pygmy retinue were richly attired and used precious stones as lamps. The king feasted his human guests sumptuously from cups studded with jewels and vessels of gold and crystal. When the guests returned to the human world, however, they found to their horror that 200 years had gone by, everyone they had known was long dead and they could no longer even understand the language. This story is one of the earliest examples of the belief that time runs strangely in fairyland.

Hidden Treasures

German medieval tales were riddled with the lore of dwarfs and dragons, magic and witchcraft. Mountain dwarfs were described as metalworkers of supernatural skill, ruled by kings whose subterranean palaces were richly stored with gold and jewels. An example is a 13th-century story of Laurin, a dwarf king. Ruling among the mountains of the Tyrol, he had a paradisal rose-garden, its boundary marked by a single silken thread. Two formidable heroes of German legend, Dietrich of Bern and Witege, penetrated the garden. King Laurin (the name means 'cunning') invited them to feast with him, drugged their wine and held them prisoner until they eventually escaped. Today, Laurin and his rose-garden are associated with Castle Tirolo in the Italian Tyrol, near Merano. This 12th-century fortress of the Counts of Tyrol was later owned by the Hapsburgs.

The *Nibelungenlied*, written down by an unknown poet in Austria in the 13th century and based on legends found in Snorri Sturluson's *Prose Edda* and other Norse sources, tells of a fierce dwarf-lord named Alberich ('elf-king'). Despite his diminutive size and advanced age – he is old, with a grey beard – he has no hesitation in challenging the mighty human hero Siegfried. He is armed with a golden scourge from which hang seven massive balls, with which he strikes such fierce blows that the hero has some difficulty in subduing him. Alberich hates Siegfried, who has earlier stolen both his treasure and his magic cloak of invisibility. In another medieval story, *Das Lied vom Hürnen Seyfrid*, the dwarf king Eugel, son of Niblung, explains to Siegfried that he and his dwarfs live in terror of a vicious giant named Kuperan, who has seized their mountain home in alliance with a dragon. Siegfried frees them by killing both the giant and the dragon, and walks off with their treasure. Both stories preserve the link between dwarfs and fabulous treasures in mountain caves and deep in the earth (a theme later adopted by Wagner for his opera cycle).

Left
A subterranean metalworker forges magical weapons

Above
The dwarf-lord Alberich is outwitted by Wotan and Loge

HELP OR HINDRANCE

All through the Middle Ages and on into modern times European beliefs and superstitions flourished about the little people, under a bewildering variety of guises. In Norway, for instance, the spirits of the countryside could be called by names meaning hidden people, those underground, people of the burial mounds or people of the hills. Helpful if demanding house and farmyard spirits included the *nisse* in Denmark, eastern and southern Norway and southern Sweden, and the *tomte* or *tomten* of northern Sweden.

These little child-sized beings, dressed in grey or brown jerkins with pointed or tasselled red or grey caps and heavy wooden clogs, were immensely strong, and fond of horses and cattle, which they helped to tend. They were also mischievous, liable to let the cows loose or toss the hay about in the barn or tease the milkmaids. To keep them sweet, it was the custom to put porridge, cakes and beer out for them on Thursday evenings and on Christmas Eve.

It was the *nisse* who held the family's luck in his hands and if he left, he might take the luck with him. On the other hand, it would not be easy to get rid of him. A Danish story tells of a man who grew so tired of his *nisse's* tricks that he decided to move house. Packing up all his belongings and loading them on a cart, he was dismayed to see the *nisse* sitting in a tub on the cart. 'So,' said the *nisse* with his characteristic horse-laugh, 'we are moving today.' The same tale appears in England, too, and elsewhere in Europe.

LITTLE-GNOME FACT

Early English contained the adjective aelfsciene, meaning 'beautiful as an elf', and down into Christian times Anglo-Saxons would give their children names beginning with aelf or alf to attract favourable elfin influences. The name of Alfred the Great, for instance, means 'elf-counsel'. On the other hand, the word aelfsiden meant 'nightmare' (and a related modern German word for nightmare is *alp*) and in the epic poem *Beowulf* elves are mentioned as evil beings. Lumbago, inflammation of the eyes, the stitch and hiccoughs were all attributed to the attentions of elves.

RIGHT
A Swedish tomte *shares a meal with his pig*

ABOVE
A little apprehensive, this Norwegian nisse *enjoys his Christmas feast*

LEFT
A goblin wakens Burd Isabel from her slumbers in the Scottish ballad

BELOW
Equipped with various implements, gnomes are often ready to lend a hand around the house and garden

There is even a story of a Scotsman named Callum, from the Lochaber district, who emigrated to America, leaving his bauchan or tricksy attendant spirit behind (or so he thought), only to find when he reached his plot of land in the New World that his first greeting was from the irrepressible bauchan, in the guise of a goat. 'Ha, ha, Callum,' it said, 'I am before you.'

In central and northern England and in Scotland the brownies played a similar role. The brownies of the Scots Border were described as small men about three feet high, dressed in ragged brown clothes, who came out at night and finished any work that had been left undone in house, stable or barn. There are stories of a brownie helpfully bringing the midwife to his pregnant human mistress when she went into labour unexpectedly. But they were also mischievous, and a favourite brownie trick was to hide all the household keys. They played a socially useful role because they were known to dislike and punish laziness and sluttishness about the house, while their pinching fingers could account for bruises and marks which maidservants might not be too keen to explain otherwise. The prudent housewife would make her brownie a nice honey-cake or leave a bowl of cream out for him. It was not done to go looking for him or openly offer him a reward, which would offend him.

In Herefordshire the household brownie was often accustomed to sit in a curve in the iron bar that hung over the fire to hang pots and kettles from, and if there was no curve people would suspend a horseshoe upside down from the bar to give the brownie a warm roost. At the old Holman Clavel Inn on the Blackdown Hills in Somerset, the resident hob or brownie, known as Charlie, used to perch comfortably on the massive beam above the fireplace. He was still remembered with affection by the locals in the 1960s.

Above
These Swedish fellows are a shining example of the gnome's traditional affinity for animals

Little-Gnome Fact
The adoption of the name brownie for junior girl guides is testimony to the creatures' generally good reputation, but there were particularly mischievous brownies, which played tricks very much like those of a poltergeist – throwing things about, mysteriously moving furniture, causing crockery to jump off the shelf and smash. Again, they could not be got rid of simply by moving house.

Below
A proliferation of gnomic attractions in England's west country means you are always assured of a warm welcome; this cheerful soul greets visitors to Padstow in Cornwall

What's in a Name?

Brownies were also called boggarts, bauchans, bogans or bugganes, hobs or lobs. Lancashire boggarts were described as about knee high, with wizened faces and scrawny necks, impudent grins and arms and legs too thin for their corpulent bodies. In a temper their faces twisted violently with rage.

Similar beings in Wales were called *bwcas* or *bwbachs*. There's a story of a Monmouthshire farm's resident bwca who befriended one of the girls and helped her with the household chores. She used to leave a bowl of cream and some wheat bread out for him, until one night she mischievously poured some stale urine into his cream. Next morning, furious, he attacked her, kicking her all over the house until she shrieked for help; he then flounced off to live at a neighbouring farm. In the Isle of Man the brownie's equivalent was the fenodoree – big, ugly, stupid, hairy and enormously strong. One of them met the local blacksmith one night and wanted to shake hands. The blacksmith cautiously held out the iron sock of a plough he was carrying and the fenodoree gripped it and twisted it almost out of shape before saying in a satisfied tone, 'There's some strong Manxmen in the world yet.'

Today's garden gnome is not expected to help with chores or punish sluttishness in the home, but he often does play something of the traditional role of supernatural household attendant, guardian and family luck-bringer performed by brownies and similar spirits in northern Europe.

Triumphant Pixies

The south-west of England was inhabited by the pixies or pigsies, or in Cornwall piskies (or piskeys), whose territory lay west of the River Parrett in Somerset. Acccording to one tradition, the pixies won a pitched battle against the fairies and drove them across the river, and certainly this is now the area in which England's gnome tourist attractions are clustered (see pages 89–103), while the garden gnome here is often the garden pixy.

Pixies could be helpful to humans, but they liked to play tricks, especially by leading travellers astray. They loved to dance or ride horses wildly at night, in circles, so forming fairy rings, and they were small enough for 20 of them to mount a single horse. Down into the 19th century on Dartmoor, they were said to gather to revel by moonlight at New Bridge on the River Dart. The Pixies' House is a cave at Sheepstor in Devon, where offerings were left for them. Dartmoor pixies also provided an explanation for oddities in the construction of a house – a bit of natural rock showing in a corner, for instance, or an odd hole in a wall, left for them to go in and out by.

Housewives often left a bowl of water out at night by the fire for the pixies to drink, and they would sometimes repay the favour by dropping a coin in the bowl.

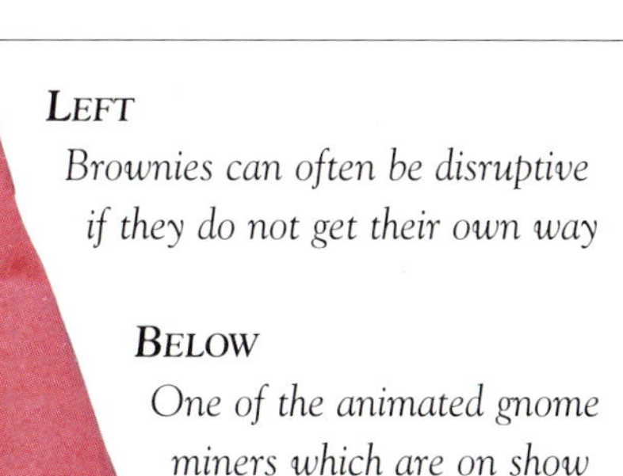

Left
Brownies can often be disruptive if they do not get their own way

Below
One of the animated gnome miners which are on show at Gnomeland in Devon

Like brownies, pixies could attach themselves to an individual household and make themselves useful. A Somerset story tells of a farmer whose resident pixies used to thrash corn for him, until one night his wife peeped through the keyhole of the barn and saw them at work, squinting and hairy, naked and cold. Taking pity on them, she made them clothes, which she left for them on the threshing floor. This may have been a mistake as they did no more work after that. Later the local church hung a set of bells in its tower and the farmer met the chief of the pixies in one of his fields. The pixy asked to borrow packhorses, so they could move themselves and their belongings away from the sound of the bells, which was troubling them. The kindly farmer lent his old horses – when they came back, they looked like two-year-olds.

In 1890 a local paper reported that a group of labourers had been working in a wood near Torrington in north Devon when one of them went to fetch a tool he had left some way away. Stooping to pick it up, he felt extremely strange and could not straighten up again. Then he heard peals of harsh laughter and realised that he had been

RIGHT
'Many gnomes a-coming' in The Book of Fairy Poetry *by Warwick Goble, and many other creatures besides*

spellbound by pixies. He managed to crawl away, though he had lost all sense of direction and did not know where he was going until he fell into a stream. When he eventurally got home, his wife told him he was a fool and should have turned his pocket inside out, which every sensible person knew would counter pixy magic.

In 1961 a woman recalled being pixy-led in a wood near Budleigh Salterton, Devon. She could not find her way out of the wood and went round and round helplessly until someone found her; then she could not understand how she had missed the path, which was in plain view, but she was told that others had been pixy-led in that wood before.

LITTLE-GNOME FACT

People who got lost in a wood or went astray at night and became hopelessly bemused were said to be pixy-led (which is the origin of the slang term 'pixillated' for drunk).

Fairies and Changelings

In Somerset the main defences against being pixy-led were to turn your coat inside out or carry a 'wicken cross' of two willow twigs. In her book on Somerset folklore, Ruth Tongue recalled how on Hallowe'en in 1943 an old farmer's wife on Exmoor sent her to bring her husband in from a nearby field one night. 'She gave me a wicken cross to carry. I found him quite bewildered in the middle of his own field, though the gate was plain to see in the moonshine. I heard nothing, but he was plagued by the sound of pixy laughter. After I had given him the cross he recovered himself and came back quite readily.'

As late as 1965 it was reported that there were elderly people living in the neigbourhood of Warleggan in Cornwall who preferred not to venture far at night for fear of being piskie-led by the wavering lights on the moors. The tradition of the piskies' eldritch laughter at the plight of travellers they had led astray accounts for the Cornish expression 'to laugh like a piskey' for a person much given to immoderate laughter, and some people were still putting a dish of cream out for the piskies well into this century. In older times a baby's nightdress was often fastened to its cradle to stop the piskies stealing the child, and in 1843 a nasty case was reported from Penzance of a farmer brutally ill-treating one of his children, whom he and his wife believed was a changeling. The arrival of a retarded child was sometimes explained by saying that it was a changeling.

The dread of changelings also appears in *The Secret Commonwealth of Elves, Fauns and Fairies*, produced in 1691 by the Scottish Presbyterian minister of Aberfoyle, Robert Kirk. This major book on the fairy beliefs of the area bordering the Scottish Lowlands and Highlands, was not published until 1815. Kirk collected traditional lore from the locals in the area and he seems to have believed that the fairy people were real. He describes how they lived in the hollow hills and could sometimes be heard inside, busy striking with hammers or baking bread. People gifted with second sight had seen them sharing human food at banquets and funeral feasts, invisible to the other guests, and some Highlanders consequently preferred not to eat anything on such occasions. They have their own chieftains, but no religion, and their women do fine spinning and embroidery. When Robert Kirk died in 1692 and his corpse was found lying on a fairy mound at Aberfoyle, it was widely believed that the minister had been taken by the fairies in whom he had shown such a persistent and perilous interest.

Regional Variations

Some fairy folk were intensely dangerous. In Wales there were vicious female mountain spirits called gwyllion, who sometimes took the form of goats and delighted in leading travellers perilously astray on mountain roads. In the North of England, according to tradition, there were evil black dwarfs called duergars – solitary, silent and icily hostile to humans. Strongly built, though no higher than a man's knee, a duergar wore moleskin trousers, a lambskin coat and a hat made of green moss decorated with a pheasant's feather. The Border redcaps, too, who lurked in old pele towers and castles where the memory of bloody deeds still lingered, were hideously dangerous. They looked like short, thickset old men with long teeth and hair, wearing red caps.

The Dutch redcaps (*kaboutermannekin*) were friendlier and more like brownies, and the Swiss dwarfs, called 'earth-men', helped with work on the farm and were good at finding animals that had strayed in the mountains. German house spirits called *kobolds* included the *biersal*, who lived in the cellar and kept the bottles and jugs clean provided a jug of beer was left out for him every day. Another variety of *kobold* lived underground in caves and mines. They looked like dwarfish old men. Sometimes they were friendly and made knocking noises to lead miners to fresh veins of ore, but they could also be mischievous or positively malignant.

Above
Arthur Rackham's mischievous goblins wreak havoc in Kensington Gardens

Left
This German mining dwarf looks a little lost, despite a lantern to lead the way

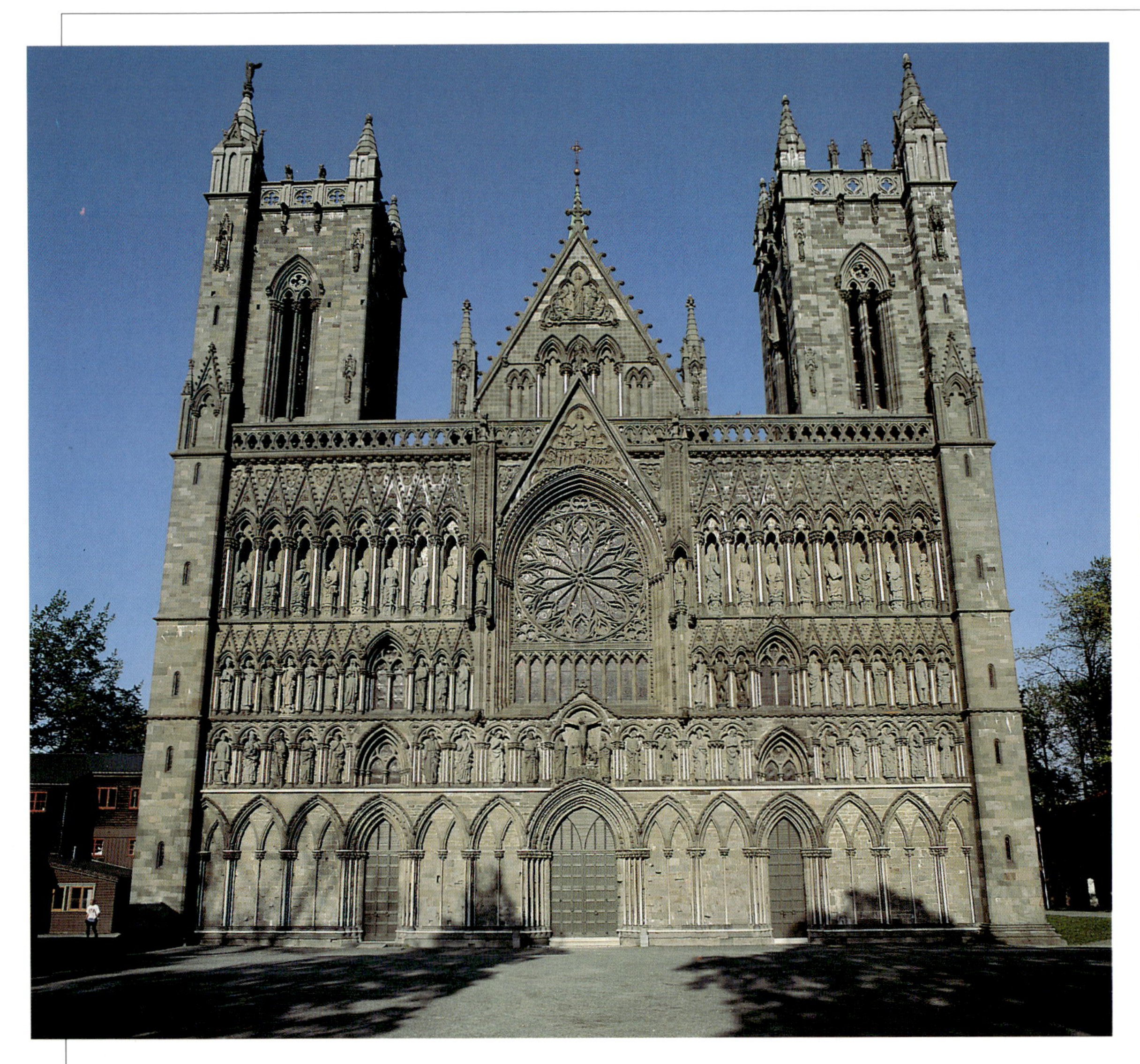

Above
It is hard to believe that trolls, those traditionally ugly, stupid creatures of Norse mythology, could possibly have built Trondheim Cathedral, left

Kobold became *gobelin* in French and goblin in English, generally meaning a malevolent spirit. *Kobold* is also the origin of cobalt, which German miners named after the mine-imp because it was so tricky to use. The 16th-century German scientist Georg Agricola, author of pioneering works on mineralogy, wrote of spirits which lived and worked in mines and could often be heard, though somehow no palpable trace of their operations could ever be found. Much given to laughing and giggling, he said, and generally helpful, they were similar to resident household spirits.

The Scandinavian trolls were originally the giants of Norse mythology, huge, ugly and impenetrably stupid brutes, like animated mountains. St Olaf, the Norwegian king who was a major force in the establishment of Christianity in the North in the 11th century, took over the role of the pagan god Thor as the trolls' great enemy in popular lore. He was said to have tricked one of them into building Norway's most famous church for him – Trondheim Cathedral.

In subsequent centuries the trolls passed gradually out of any connection with the real world and into the realm of fantasy. Some were said to be of mountainous proportions, wih only one eye or three heads and a disquieting appetite for human flesh. They were attracted to human women and a recurrent theme of medieval ballads in Norway, Sweden and Denmark is of the troll who comes to the king's palace and carries off his beautiful daughter. The king's knights are scared of the troll and the princess is saved by a young page at the court, of whom no one has previously taken any notice, who gallantly rescues her from the troll's perilous mountain realm and wins her hand in marriage.

Other trolls shrank in size, sometimes to dwarfish proportions, and joined the hidden folk, though they were still exceptionally ugly, malicious and dangerous inhabitants of hills, rocks and caves. There is a Danish story of a plague of them – dwarfish, hunch-backed and long-nosed, in grey jerkins and red caps – infesting an area until the church bell was rung, when they all promptly decamped.

In the Shetland Islands and the Orkneys, the trolls turned into trows, small creatures who lived underground and always walked backwards when observed by human beings.

It was very unlucky to see a trow and they were generally feared, though there were rumours of them sometimes taking a family under their protection. They dressed in grey and were fond of playing the fiddle.

Traditions can resonate down the years in unexpected ways. In 1996 in England, anti-motorway protestors opposing the construction of a new bypass between Honiton and Exeter in south Devon built a camp on a hilltop in the style of an Iron Age hillfort and dug an extensive network of underground tunnels. They called it Trollheim, 'troll-home'.

Going Underground

The mining spirits of Welsh tradition were the coblynau, about a foot and a half high and grotesquely ugly. They would throw showers of small stones at human miners who upset them, but they were generally kindly and the knocking sounds they made led the way to rich finds. In the north-east of England and the Newcastle collieries in the 1770s, local miners told of similar traditions.

In the tin mines of Cornwall the resident spirits were called knockers, nuggies, nickers, buccas or gathorns, and described as diminutive old men with big heads and clumsy arms and legs. Heard, but seldom seen, they kept busy with their own mining operations. It was widely believed they were responsible for the strange flickering lights (actually caused by natural gas) which the miners thought showed the way to rich lodes of ore.

The spirits were generally friendly to human miners, but they could be spiteful and pelt a miner who was disrespectful to them or disbelieved in them with a shower of small stones. It was important never to annoy them by whistling or swearing, or especially by making the sign of the cross or marking anything in the mine with a cross, which would seriously upset them. Other underground beings of Cornish lore were the spriggans, who guarded buried treasures and lived in prehistoric cromlechs and burial barrows.

The formidable fairy folk of Ireland, the side (pronounced 'shee'), also lived inside prehistoric burial mounds. Normally invisible, they could be seen by mortals on Midsummer Eve or by those with second sight. Irish household spirits, which would help with the chores of kitchen and stableyard, were called pookas or phookas, while the bibulous, red-nosed cluricaune lived in the wine cellar and scared servants who tried to steal the wine. He wore a red nightcap and a leather apron. Leprechauns, meanwhile, were solitary little elfin shoemakers, usually seen working on a single shoe only, and generally described as cheerful, wrinkled, bearded and bespectacled little men, wearing a red or green coat with large, shiny buttons, knee breeches, a red or green night-cap or a three-cornered hat, and a long leather apron. Beside them would usually be a small pipe or a pitcher of beer.

Left
This colourful leprechaun from across the Irish sea has taken a break from his labours with a pitcher of beer

Above
Usually seen in the company of his friends playing the mandolin and the fiddle, this concertina player makes up a trio of young musical leprechauns

THE LITTLE PEOPLE

SPECIAL FEATURES & SUBTLE DIFFERENCES

Paracelsus called the earth spirits 'pygmies' or alternatively 'gnomes', which he may have coined from Greek genomus or 'earth-dweller'. 'The gnomes', he said, 'have minds, but no souls, and so are incapable of spiritual development. They stand about two feet tall, but can expand themselves to huge size at will, and live in underground houses and palaces. Adapted to their element, they can breathe, see and move as easily underground as fish do in water. Gnomes have bodies of flesh and blood, they speak and reason, they eat and sleep and propagate their species, fall ill and die. They sometimes take a liking to a human being and enter his service, but are generally hostile to humans.'

LEFT
Strange rock formations were frequently explained as trolls turned to stone, but this stony chap looks more like a pixie or elf

Many Scandinavian myths feature dwarfs, who were famed for their craftsmanship and mastery of magic runes and spells. According to legend, living underground or in rocks, dwarfs could not face the sun, whose rays would turn them to stone.

Pixies had red hair, pointed ears and turned-up noses, and often suffered from a squint – and they dressed all in green.

Fairies share the dress and speech of the area in which they live. They are much longer lived than mortals and are immune to disease, but eventually dwindle and fade away into death.

LEFT
Trolls feared thunder, the sign of the cross and the sound of church bells – the pagan god Thor and Christianity, in other words

BELOW & RIGHT
Leprechauns knew the whereabouts of buried treasure and in theory they could be forced to reveal what they knew, but the leprechaun was skilled at tricking his human captor into looking elswhere for a moment, when he would vanish in a flash

BELOW
Regular sacrifices were still being offered to the elves in the 11th century in Scandinavia, and elves were often linked in popular belief with the dead in their burial mounds. In Sweden ancient cup-shaped marks on rocks and stone tombs have been filled with milk as a simple offering to elves even into the 20th century

BELOW
Today's gnomes come in all shapes and sizes, but are invariably cheery fellows

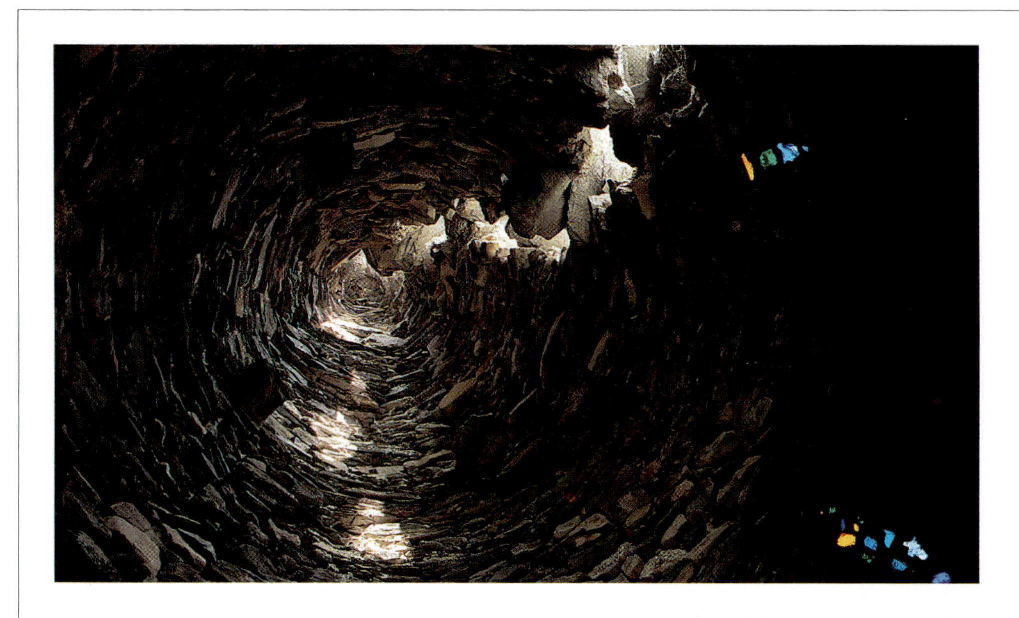

Irish and other European emigrants to the New World naturally took their traditions of the little people with them, and American leprechauns were believed to live under mushrooms and toadstools or beneath fallen trees. There were fairy rings on both sides of the Atlantic and tales of people being pixie-led. The tooth fairy also made the ocean crossing successfully.

THE GNOME IS BORN

Popular tradition in Europe knew of a wide variety of diminutive beings. It was not until the 16th century, however, that the word 'gnome' appeared for the first time, apparently coined by the German physician and alchemist Paracelsus (1493–1541). Born in Switzerland at Einsiedeln, near Zurich, and rejoicing in the name Philippus Aureolus Theophrastus Bombast von Hohenheim, he called himself Paracelsus to show that he was immeasurably the superior of Celsus, the revered Roman medical writer of the 1st century.

Paracelsus attended numerous universities, holding the professors and courses in complete contempt, and spent some time at Sigismund Fugger's metallurgical workshops in the Tyrol. Here he decided that silicosis, the miners' disease, was not inflicted by diminutive mine-spirits, as was generally believed, but was caused by inhaling metal vapours. He travelled widely, hobnobbing with alchemists, occultists and gypsies, and gaining a reputation for achieving almost miraculous cures.

Paracelsus was an unruly and tempestuous genius, boastful, quarrelsome and frequently drunk. Although now hailed as one of the founders of modern scientific medicine, he was also a man of his time, accepting the prevailing theory of the four elements – fire, air, water and earth – as the basis of matter. Each element supposedly had its own resident spirits, and Paracelsus identified the earth-spirits of intellectual theory with the dwarfs and mining fairies of popular belief.

ABOVE LEFT
Sneem village, in Ireland's County Kerry, is the site of the mysterious Ring of Kerry; inside, shown by shafts of light, is the Way the Fairies Went

LEFT
The word gnome is attributed to the alchemist Paracelsus

Rewards and Fairies

Farewell, rewards and fairies,
Good housewives now may say,
For now foul sluts in dairies
Do fare as well as they.
For though they sweep their
  hearths no less
Than maids were wont to do,
Yet who of late for cleanliness
Finds sixpence in her shoe?

Richard Corbet
'The Fairies' Farewell'

IF YOU ARE SITTING COMFORTABLY...

BY THE MID-18TH CENTURY Paracelsus' gnomes, the four elements and their attendant spirits had vanished from educated people's picture of the real world, surviving only as a literary conceit. At the same time traditional European folk beliefs about the little people had been seriously weakened with the rise of modern science. There was now to develop, however, a strong resurgence of intellectual interest in the old traditions in northern Europe, often linked with rising nationalism.

ABOVE
The mythical Lorelei mourns on the rock which bears her name

RIGHT
Story time with Jacob and Wilhelm, the brothers Grimm

In the early 1800 s at Heidelberg two poets and friends, Ludwig Joachim von Arnim and Clemens Brentano, published more than 700 German folk songs (as *Des Knaben Wunderhorn*). Some they collected on a journey made along the Rhine, but most of their material did not come directly from oral sources and they 'improved' five out of every six of their songs, while Brentano actually invented the legend of the Lorelei, the beautiful siren of the Rhine whose enticing singing lured boatmen on the river to their deaths.

Von Arnim and Brentano dedicated their first volume to Goethe and their collection was an instant success. Germany at this time was a patchwork of many kingdoms and states, developing and searching for a German identity. Songs and stories handed down over generations of simple German 'folk' were thought to contain a true German-ness which the sophisticated productions of educated, Europeanised intellectuals were bound to lack. They were an expression of what German intellectuals of the time liked to call the 'folk-soul'. Von Arnim and Brentano were friends of the Brothers Grimm, the most formidable figures in this field, who are regarded today as the founders of the modern study of folklore. The two brothers, Jacob (1785–1863) and Wilhelm (1786–1859), were born at Hanau in central Germany, where their father, who died when they were children, was town clerk. They lived and worked closely together all their lives, making prolific contributions to the study of the German language and Germanic mythology. In 1812 they began publishing their Kinder- und Hausmärchen, later to appear in hundreds of editions in over 70 languages and gain fame in English as *Grimms' Fairy Tales*.

GRIMM BY NAME...

The stories included versions of familiar favourites such as *Cinderella* and *Little Red Riding Hood* as well as *Hansel and Gretel*, *Rapunzel*, the *Frog Prince* and *Rumpelstiltskin*. There was also the tale of Snow White (or Snowdrop) and the queen, her evil stepmother. Intensely jealous of Snow White's beauty, the queen orders one of her men to kill the girl in the forest, but he takes pity on her and leaves her there. Lost and afraid, Snow White comes to a neat little house, with seven little beds and seven places set at a small table for a meal.

The house belongs to seven dwarfs, who spend their days busily digging for ore in the mountains. They are kind to Snow White and she keeps house for them. In the end she is saved from her stepmother's murderous machinations by a handsome prince and they live happily ever after, while the evil queen is made to put on a pair of red-hot iron shoes, specially heated for the purpose, in which she dances frantically until she falls dead.

This last cruel incident is usually bowdlerised away, but artists from George Cruikshank to Arthur Rackham and Walt Disney's animators have delighted in drawing the dwarfs in a variety of styles.

ABOVE & BELOW
Seven concerned dwarfs gather round the stricken Snow White in the traditional scene, while their modern counterparts look on

RIGHT
The servant discovers Rumpelstiltskin deep in the forest

TALES OF OLD AND NEW

The little people of Germanic tradition appear again in *The Elves and the Shoemaker*. Beatrix Potter would later come across a version of this story in Gloucestershire: she turned it into *The Tailor of Gloucester*, with mice taking the place of the elves.

In the Rumpelstiltskin story, a miller's beautiful daughter is given an impossible task by the king: spin gold out of straw and be his queen, or be put to death. She is saved by a strange little mannikin who does the spinning for her on condition that she gives him her first child (again reminiscent of the changeling theme). When the time comes for her to keep her bargain he relents and gives her three days to guess his name or he will take the child. The miller's daughter tries every manner of odd name she can think of, beginning with Timothy, Benjamin and Jeremiah, and going on to Bandylegs, Hunchback and Crookshanks, all in vain.

Then at last, a servant she has sent to scour the country for strange names comes to a little hut in the forest and sees the cunning dwarf dancing round the fire, gleefully singing his name – Rumpelstiltskin. The servant hurries back to report to the queen and the dwarf is thwarted.

The story of Rumpelstiltskin is known in a wide range of different versions all over Europe, with the character's name varying from one country to another: he is known as Gillitrut in Sweden; Ricdin-Ricdon in France; Trit-a-Trot in Ireland; Terrytop or Whuppity Stoorie in Scotland; Trwtyn-Tratyn in Wales. And, according to a version told in Suffolk, and another version heard as recently as 1992 in Liverpool, the little 'creature' of the story is called Tom Tit Tot.

BELOW
This sturdy fellow would perhaps have spent his time crawling along mine shafts at the turn of the century

NATIONAL IDENTITY

The Brothers Grimm collected much more material straight from the mouths of peasant story-tellers, clarifying and 'improving' the originals. The brothers believed that the stories and traditions they gathered were expressions of the fundamental German spirit. The tales were not intended for children's consumption and the brothers came to regret putting the word 'children' in their original title. In their own time, however, the brothers galvanised the study of traditional lore, tales and songs all over Europe.

Kobolds seen in mine workings are described as old men about ten inches tall with long beards, dressed like miners with white hoods and carrying picks, hammers and lanterns. They could be helpful to human miners, but liked to tease them and sometimes knocked three times to presage a miner's death. In the German mines at Idrija in Slovenia, the miners used to put food out regularly for the *kobolds* and once a year bought a child's red coat as a present for them. If they failed to do this, they believed, the *kobolds* would be angry and cause them harm. Many of these traditions came from the mountain and mining region on the border of Bohemia (subsequently Czechoslovakia and now the Czech Republic).

BELOW
These cheeky little dwarf miners have no need for clothes while working deep in the underground chambers

ABOVE
Lanterns are useful for venturing abroad when humans are asleep

RIGHT
Proud of his mining heritage, this figure stands atop a mountain of rubble commemorating 111 years of garden dwarfs

In Norway, which in 1814 escaped from centuries under the rule of Denmark, independence spurred nationalists to search for a distinctive Norwegian identity and national spirit which, as in Germany, were found in peasant folk traditions. Pioneer folklorists Peter Christian Asbjörnsen and Jörgen Moe collected popular tales from rural Norway and published them in the 1840s. The stories were hailed as coming from the depths of the folk-soul, intimately connected with the unspoiled beauty of the Norwegian landscape with its mountains, forests and fjords, and with the 'pure' Norwegian still spoken in country areas, in contrast to the Danish-influenced language of educated people. An obvious difficulty here was that the plots and motifs of so many of the tales, far from being confined to Norway, were also common to a number of other European countries, but nationalists liked to think that the peasant traditions of individual regions put their own distinctive stamp on the common stock.

RIGHT
Peter Christian Asbjörnsen was a great exponent of Norwegian Folk Tales and Songs

Asbjörnsen's mother had been psychic and every now and again saw ghosts and spirits from beneath the ground, and he had heard many traditional stories of the fairy folk from the workers in his father's glazing workshop. His friend Moe, a poet, became Norway's first folklore academic as a research fellow in the subject, and their collection of folk tales influenced Ibsen.

Another country where nationalism and the study of folk tradition went hand in hand was Ireland. Thomas Crofton Croker's, Fairy Legends and Traditions of the South of Ireland, published in 1825, was Great Britain's first field collection and was promptly translated into German by the Grimms (as 'Irish Elftales'). Other writers soon dipped their pens in the rich wells of Irish country lore and later in the century the rediscovery of Irish Celtic mythology and folklore was crucial to the drive to forge an Irish national identity totally independent of England.

The great poet W B Yeats (1865–1939), a key figure in the independence movement, published his own versions of Irish peasant tales and fairy tales in the late 19th century, and the Gaelic League was founded in 1893 to bring the Irish language and native story-telling, folk dances and sports back into widespread use. Similar developments also helped to bolster nationalism in Scotland and Wales.

ABOVE
An early edition of Asbjörnsen and Moe's selection of folk tales

ABOVE RIGHT
Jörgen Moe served as bishop of Christiansand from 1875 to 1881

Christmas is Coming...

The Brothers Grimm and their successors did more than record traditional material, make its study academically respectable and uncover fresh seams of inspiration for such giants as Wagner in Germany, Hans Christian Andersen in Denmark, Ibsen in Norway and Yeats in Ireland. They gave the fairy folk and little people of Northern European lore a new importance. It was not necessary to believe in them literally – though some still did – to see them as symbolic of an ancient and profound understanding of the world, preserved in the traditions of ordinary people living close to nature and the land. This helped to create the atmosphere in which the garden gnome was later to make his entrance.

Another milestone was the development of Christmas in 19th-century England, where it took a distinctly Germanic turn, partly through the influence of Prince Albert, Queen Victoria's consort. The Christmas tree, from the Rhineland area of Germany, was introduced into England by German immigrants, including well-to-do merchants settled in Manchester. Prince Albert installed Christmas trees at Windsor Castle from the 1840s onwards, and with the prestige of royal approval the custom spread rapidly. The tree's glittering lights gave it a fairyland look which the Victorians liked, and a fairy often presided at the top. Charles Dickens commended 'the pretty German toy' and a magazine writer in 1867 said that 'the little fairy tree for the little ones' was too well known to need description. It was also adopted in the United States, in Norway, Denmark and Holland, and later in Sweden and France.

Father Christmas turned into a foreigner. The Father Christmas of old England appeared in mumming plays and was imagined presiding over the season's festivities in a spirit of vague benevolence. He usually wore a holly-leaf crown, but was pictured in all sorts of different costumes and guises. Mother Christmas was occasionally mentioned, too.

Neither of them had any particular connection with children or presents, still less with jingling sleigh-bells and reindeer. By the 1870s, however, today's familiar custom of hanging up stockings on Christmas Eve for Santa Claus to fill with goodies such as fruit and sweets and had reached England. Santa Claus was an immigrant from Holland by way of North America. Originally Saint Nicholas, the patron saint of children and sailors, he crossed the Atlantic with Dutch settlers whose children put their shoes out on St Nicholas' Eve for the kindly saint to fill with small gifts.

Above & Left
Father Christmas as represented in two 19th-century illustrations

'Twas the Night Before Christmas

The custom caught on and moved to Christmas Eve, as described in a poem of 1822, 'A Visit from Saint Nicholas' (or 'The Night Before Christmas'), written for his children by Clement Clarke Moore, a respectable New York academic who was so embarrassed by its popularity that for years he refused to admit it was his.

The diminutive saint arrives on Christmas Eve in a tiny sleigh drawn by eight miniature reindeer called Dasher, Dancer, Prancer, Vixen, Comet, Cupid, Donder and Blixen (there was no red-nosed Rudolph as yet). Dressed in furs tarnished with soot and ashes from descending the chimney, he swiftly fills the children's stockings before dashing away to his next port of call. The poem describes Santa Claus as a little old elf:

His eyes how they twinkled! his dimples how merry!
His cheeks were like roses, his nose like a cherry;
His droll little mouth was drawn up like a bow,
And the beard on his chin was as white as the snow.
The stump of a pipe he held tight in his teeth,
And the smoke it encircled his head like a wreath.
He had a broad face, and a little round belly
That shook when he laughed, like bowl full of jelly.
He was chubby and plump, – a right jolly old elf –
And I laughed when I saw him, in spite of myself.

The elfin, dwarfish impression was reinforced by the popular magazine illustrations of Santa Claus drawn from the 1860s by Thomas Nast, who came from a German family.

In England Santa Claus was rapidly assimilated to Father Christmas and acquired the appearance familiar today, which is still distinctly gnome-like, with a white beard, a beaming face, apple cheeks, twinkling eyes and a red hood or tasselled cap. Though not necessarily dwarfish in size, like the dwarfs of Germanic lore he is associated with treasure – in the form of Christmas presents.

In Sweden the brownie-like house and farm spirits of folk tradition were depicted by Jenny Nyström in an 1875 children's story book as jolly little men in red stocking caps. This caught on and the *tomte* acquired a much more sentimentalised, child-friendly character than before.

Over the last hundred years or so, under the influence of authors and artists, he has blended with the Santa Claus figure to become a lovable Christmas visitor who brings presents house for small children (he is played by a friend or neighbour in costume).

The fairyland of Victorian England, with Santa Claus and the Christmas tree flourishing on its borders, was also largely the creation of authors and artists rather than 'the folk'. It reached its full growth after the first English version of stories from the Brothers Grimm were published in 1823 and the first English translation of Hans Christian Andersen's fairy tales appeared in 1846. Charles Dickens and other well-known authors wrote fairy tales, loaded with moral messages for both children and their parents, while a wishful, wistful view of childhood as a state of paradisal innocence and sweetness turned fairies into the childish little figures familiar in late Victorian and Edwardian art, flying from flower to flower on butterfly wings. While the industrial revolution ate away at the traditional beliefs about the fairy folk among country people, they flourished in a middle-class climate as desirable symbols and models for children. This, too, helped to form the climate of ideas and sentiment into which the garden gnome was born.

LEFT
Christmas Jorvik Viking style in York

BELOW
Father Christmas, presents all wrapped, relaxes with his cat in this postcard from an original illustration by Lars Carlsson

LITTLE-GNOME FACT

The word *nisse* from Scandinavian tradition is connected with the name Nils or Niels, which is linked with Nicolaus or Claus. In Denmark houses are decorated with figures of them for luck at Christmas time, wearing red hats and shirts, blue or grey trousers and clogs, while back in Britain at the Jorvik Viking Centre in York a Christmas nisse takes up residence every year in a Santa Claus capacity as a children's present-giver and story-teller.

Gnomes and Gardens

A garden is a piece of wild nature tamed and separated from the outside world as a haven of beauty, peace and harmony, where the gardener clings to the optimistic illusion of being in control. Figures of gods and other mythological beings, animals and other personifications are placed not merely as attractions for the eye, but to bring them and what they represent within the gardener's control, and so within his own psyche, as part of the harmony which he strives to create.

GARDENS OF THE HEART

IN THE ANCIENT WORLD the Greeks planted trees and shrubs in the precincts of temples and the Romans developed the art of ornamental gardening. Wealthy Romans placed statues in their gardens and the figure of a deity represented certain desired qualities. The goddess Venus, for instance, could stand for love or peace or justice and her statue, as well as being beautiful, brought these ideas into both the garden and the observer's mind and heart. The Romans also liked aviaries and water features – fountains and fish ponds and miniature cascades – and they used topiary, or 'barbered groves' as they called them, to create figures of animals, fleets of ships, hunting scenes and pleasing designs, clipped out of cypress and box.

RIGHT
This west-country gnome looks a little too young to drink

BELOW
No gathering of gnomes would be complete without a toadstool to sit around

When the Renaissance dawned in Italy with its passionate enthusiasm for the civilisation of Ancient Greece and Rome, no classical Roman garden survived to be copied, but descriptions by Pliny and other writers were used to lay out gardens in the antique taste, with statuary playing a prominent part. In the 16th-century garden of the Villa d'Este at Tivoli, with its spectacular fountains and water features, a figure of Hercules stands between the Grove of Venus and the Grove of Diana to symbolise the choice between erotic love and chastity, or pleasure and restraint, while water spouts from the breasts of sculpted goddesses and sphinxes as symbols of fertility. Theatrical effects were created in the weird garden grove made at Bomarzo by one of the Orsini family, which contained frightening monsters, a hell-mouth and enigmatic figures to startle unwary visitors. Jokiness reigned in the Fugger dynasty's gardens at Augsburg in Bavaria, where in the 1580s ladies were lured into looking over a bridge and then unexpectedly sprayed by jets of water that drenched their legs and petticoats. Suburban gardens of today which create theatrical or humorous effects with

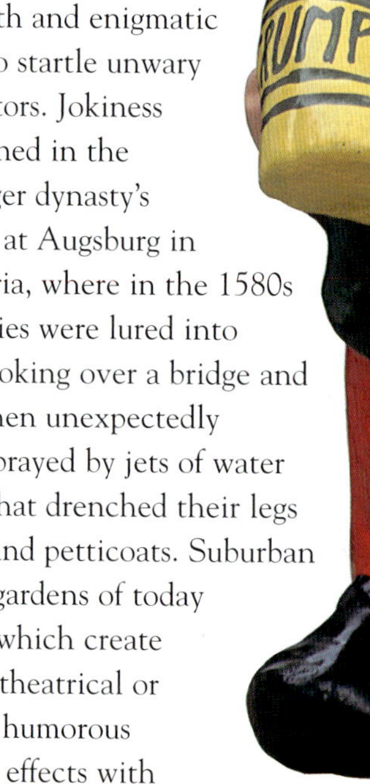

gnomes, toadstools, a pond, figures of animals, Chinese lanterns, miniature Swiss chalets and model windmills whose sails turn in the breeze are in the tradition of these majestic Renaissance gardens of popes and princes.

During the 16th and 17th centuries successive generations of the Medici family laid out and elaborated the famous Boboli Gardens in Florence. The statues here include figures of peasants, agricultural labourers, musicians and animals, and among the ranks of the classical gods is Pietro Barbino, the obese court dwarf of Cosimo I de Medici, naked and riding a giant tortoise in character as Bacchus, the Roman deity of drunkenness and wine.

COURTLY FIGURES

The court dwarf was another feature of aristocratic life in Renaissance Europe. A combination of jester and pet, he again reflected the days of imperial Rome, when slave children were sometimes deliberately stunted to fetch a good price as dwarfs. Italian princely families like the Gonzagas of Mantua kept dwarfs. Velasquez painted the dwarfs of the Spanish court; King Stanislas of Poland's dwarf, Nicholas Ferry, stood three feet high and the Russian tsars kept dwarfs in droves. Charles I of England had a court dwarf named Jeffrey Hudson, a butcher's son from Oakham in Rutland, who at the age of nine, perfectly formed but scarcely eighteen inches tall, had entered the grand household of the Duchess of Buckingham. She liked to serve him up at the dinner table concealed in a pie, from which he emerged to perform lively antics. He amused Charles I's French queen, Henrietta Maria, who took him off to court. A vigorous fellow, he grew to be something between three feet six and three feet nine inches tall, and lived into his sixties.

ABOVE
Van Dyck's portrait of c1633 shows Queen Henrietta Maria with her favourite dwarf-child Jeffrey Hudson

ABOVE LEFT & LEFT
Court dwarf Pietro Barbino portrays Bacchus at the Boboli Gardens, while, left, one of the Salzburg statues looks rather unwell

Crude but Popular

Court dwarfs probably helped to inspire an early 18th-century vogue in northern Italy and southern Germany for grotesque garden statues known as *gobbi* (Italian for hunchbacks) or *callotti* to link them with the French artist Jacques Callot, (c1592–1635), who, in 1616 had published a set of 20 engravings of dwarf hunchbacks and cripples, costumed as comedy actors, musicians, dancers, jesters and beggars. The idea was later appropriated by Johann Andreas Pfeffer, a German publisher, who in Vienna in 1706 produced a book of copper engravings based on Callot's originals, but somewhat cruder, in which dwarfs posed as fashionable ladies and gentlemen and professional people, ridiculously overdressed and making affected gestures to invite the onlooker's amused contempt.

Dwarf garden figures, copied from or inspired by these illustrations, were popular in northern Italy at this time and the Villa Valmarana near Vicenza was known as 'the villa with the dwarfs' for the figures on its garden walls. They also appeared in gardens in Austria and the south of Germany, in Bohemia and Bavaria, often positioned on terraces or along the tops of walls and balustrades. A notable group of them survives in the Hofgarten at Öttingen, near Nördlingen in Bavaria, at the former residence of the local princes. An orchestra of dwarfs makes silent music in the garden at Schloss Sinning, near Neuburg, while at the castle at Weikersheim the staff of the Counts of Hohenlohe are caricatured as dwarf drummers and gardeners. At Salzburg in Austria a 'theatre of dwarfs' was created in the gardens of Mirabell Castle, with grotesque figures of peasants and workers, some of them playing a ball game: the survivors are now in the nearby Bastion Garden.

The fashionable garden dwarfs also appeared inside people's houses, depicted in the wallpaper or as porcelain figures, in marquetry work or on stove tiles, or even in marzipan as decorations for cakes. Apart from their diminutive size, they have nothing in common with the dwarfs of folk tradition or the garden gnomes of the following century. They look quite different, they are dressed in varying contemporary styles and their purpose is cruelly satirical. They are meant to cut human beings down to size and provoke sardonic, superior mirth at their ugliness and overweening pretensions.

After the middle of the 18th century the English style of naturalistic landscaping in the Capability Brown manner became the fashionable thing in Germany.

Above
This unusual combination of baby gnome and penguin is actually a cake decoration from the 1930s

Above & Right
A few of the surviving dwarf figures from the grounds of Mirabell Castle, dating from around 1715, busy themelves with ball games

Grotesque garden dwarfs went out of style, their places taken by bouncing putti and dignified classical figures, partly because the dwarfs had been painted, which the new taste in garden statuary disliked. In his poem 'Hermann und Dorothea', written in 1797, Goethe had one of the characters speak of his garden and his delightful grotto, with its shell-work and corals and its coloured figures of dwarfs and stone beggars, once the centre of admiration, now half-ruined and considered completely old hat.

A QUESTION OF TASTE

In the Victorian age, English gardening reacted against the elegant simplicity of Georgian and Regency taste and burst out in a riot of spectacle and colour. There were exciting new imported plants, and gardeners delighted in flower beds blazing with colour, ornamental shrubs and trees in weird shapes and improbable hues, terraces brightly paved with coloured stones, mysterious grottoes, fanciful ferneries and arrangements of gnarled tree stumps and writhing roots, fake Swiss bridges, Japanese frogs and cranes, Chinese pagodas. Topiary came back into its own, rockeries catered to an enthusiasm for alpines and a zeal to create imitations of mountain scenery, and there was a liking for 'rustic' sheds, bridges and garden seats, using wood with the bark left on and with real or simulated knotholes and stumps. Sir Charles Isham's rockery and its attendant gnomes fitted in perfectly, but his three daughters evidently found the gnomes embarrassing and had them removed after their father's death in 1903. He had no son and Lamport Hall passed to a cousin. (See pages 38–9).

Meanwhile, German ceramics firms were starting to make *gartenzwergen*, or 'garden dwarfs' (not gnomes), for outdoor use. The Heissner company at Gräfenroda, near Erfurt in Hesse, which from 1871 turned out quantities of indoor dwarfs holding forks, spades, pipes or harmonicas, as well as figures of deer, boars, bears and lynxes in terracotta or coloured plaster, had begun to manufacture garden dwarfs by about 1900. Advertisements by Ludwig Möller's garden emporium in Erfurt offer *gnomen-figuren* for the garden, standing, seated or reclining, dressed in rustic jerkins and aprons with red or brown caps, holding baskets, axes, spades, rakes, rabbits, shotguns or beer mugs, or smoking pipes. They are apple-cheeked, amply bearded, traditional peasant figures, smiling or solemn, not the grotesque caricatures of the 18th century. In his novel *Felix Krull*, set in about 1900, Thomas Mann described a Rhineland villa garden of the time, liberally stocked with dwarfs, toadstools, a distorting mirror, a tinkling Aeolian harp and a pool seemingly alive with silver fish.

LEFT
This painted brass gnome with umbrella is a more unusual example from Victorian times

RIGHT
Standing 3ft 3in (1m) tall and made by the Austrian State Pottery, this gnome dates from 1718–1861

THE GNOMES OF LAMPORT HALL

THE ORIGINAL BRITISH STATELY GNOMES

It was not until the 19th century, after the Brothers Grimm had created a new interest in the dwarfs and *kobolds* of old Germanic tradition, that dwarf figures of the folklore type were manufactured in Germany – not for gardens, but as indoor ornaments. They could also serve as footstools or they might work miniature cannon for lighting cigars. Some of them, on sale in Nuremberg in Bavaria and designed to stand on dinner tables, caught the eye of an eccentric English country gentleman, Sir Charles Isham of Lamport Hall in Northamptonshire.

Charles Edmund Isham had inherited his stately ancestral pile and his baronetcy after the suicide of his elder brother in 1846. A zealous gardener, he immediately devoted himself to improving the grounds and soon began the construction of a notable rockery, 90ft long, 47ft wide and 24ft high (27 x 14 x 7m), in a crescent shape. On it he grew dwarf conifers with other miniature plants and alpines, and its dark crevices and quartz-lined little caves which sparkled in the sunlight up struck him as an eminently suitable home for a population of dwarfs. He began installing German indoor figures outdoors in the rockery in the 1860s and thereby became the father of the garden gnome.

The name 'gnome' for the dwarf figures seems to have been a mistake by Sir Charles. His German imports were probably sold to him as *gnomen-figuren*, meaning 'miniature figures', but he took this to mean figures of 'gnomes'. Sadly, only one of them has survived. Kept

Above & Left
The celebrated stately gnome makes a rare foray outdoors to his grotto at Lamport Hall, left and inset

indoors in a glass case at Lamport Hall, it is said to be insured for £1 million and is the only gnome ever to be admitted into the august precincts of the Chelsea Flower Show, in 1993. Unlike the 18th-century German grotesques, the figure represents a dwarf from traditional folklore. Standing about 4 inches (10cm) high, he wears a red, pointed cap with a jerkin, leggings and black clogs, and sports a bushy beard resembling Sir Charles's own.

Seeing Is Believing

Sir Charles's liking for his gnomes had a religious tinge. A high-minded vegetarian, he was interested in the supernatural. Perhaps under the influence of his brother's tragic death, he was an enthusiast for the Spiritualist Movement, which claimed to make contact with the spirits of the dead and created much excitement in England in the 1840s and 1850s, and he attended many seances. Inclined to believe in fairies, he was impressed by accounts of sightings of them in Ireland, and believed that seeing and hearing gnomes was 'not mental delusion, but an extension of faculty' (or what might now be called extrasensory perception).

He also backed a pioneer hypnotist, or 'mesmerist', named Thomas Capern, who he said had worked amazing cures in the Lamport neighbourhood. Sir Charles had a sense of humour and liked to speculate about what his gnomes might be doing when his eye was not on them. He ruled his gardens for more than 50 years.

Above
Another famous hideaway is the Elfin Oak in Kensington Gardens

Gnome Strike Action

In 1897 the rockery was written up in *Gardeners' Chronicle* magazine. One of the gnomes was lying full-length on a rock and gazing over the ledge at others apparently walking beneath, while a group of elfin miners had gone on strike. Downing their tools and wheelbarrows, they were lounging, hands in pockets, beneath a hand-lettered sign that proclaimed:

Eight hours Sleep
Eight hours Play
Eight hours Work
Eight shillings Pay

They were still in place, still on strike, when a journalist on the *Strand Magazine* wrote about the rockery in 1900. He also admired the tableaux of working gnome miners in other parts of the site, with their picks and shovels, their ladders and loaded wheelbarrows. The photographs show them in Phrygian caps. 'They compel one,' he wrote,' to imagine himself in another world.'

LEFT
Although probably well past retirement age, this sprightly fellow enjoys his work at the Gnome Reserve in Devon

ABOVE
Examples from an early German advertisement for 'gnomen-figuren'

A SHOWCASE FOR GNOMES

In 1908 the German ceramic firm of Ernst Wahliss, which had galleries in London's Oxford Street, advertised its gnomes and animal figures for the garden in the smart pages of the *Connoisseur* magazine: 'The Gnomes and quaint Manikins, which we stock in all styles and sizes, lend themselves particularly well for the artistic decoration of parks, gardens, etc. One of our clients has over one hundred of these gnomes in his famous subterranean passages and gardens.'

The client was Sir Frank Crisp, who created one of the most extraordinary gardens of the period at Friar Park, near Henley-on-Thames, and opened it to visitors (the estate today belongs to George Harrison, the former Beatle). Sir Frank was senior partner in a London firm of solicitors, and a rich man. Like Sir Charles Isham before him, he was interested in the supernatural. At Friar Park he constructed a topiary garden with figures of animals and a famous Alpine rock garden, built from 7,000 tons of stone and housing 4,000 plants. It rose to a model of the Matterhorn, capped with alabaster 'snow', and Sir Frank installed cast-iron figures of chamois at suitable vantage points. He also made five show-caves, which included a wishing-well cave with bats, owls, crocodiles and mirrors providing optical illusions, a cave with skeletons and distorting mirrors, and a cave with an illusion of a friar being electrocuted. The fifth was the Gnome Cave where, according to Sir Frank's 1906 guidebook for visitors, one group of figures was shown trying to take a baby bird and being attacked by the mother bird, a gnome was taking snuff; another was suffering from toothache (much to the amusement of his comrades) and another was 'behaving disrespectfully to a grasshopper'. One gnome was being startled by a snake and another by an exploding bottle of champagne he was trying to carry off, while at the end of the cave a distorting mirror turned the unsuspecting visitor into a gnome.

ENOUGH IS ENOUGH

This relentless jokiness no doubt hardened the hearts of the leading garden writers, who turned their faces firmly against vulgar Victorian spontaneity, variety and excess. The formidably authoritative William Robinson, who ran The Garden magazine from 1871, described Sir Frank Crisp's imitation Matterhorn at Friar Park as the best rock garden in natural stone he had ever seen, but he issued no encyclical approving Sir Frank's gnomes and he disliked the tremendous topiary garden created for Ascott, the Rothschild stately home at Wing in Buckinghamshire, with its numerous figures of animals. His preference was for naturalistic gardens in which native English plants were grown in an apparently unplanned manner. He disliked obvious artifice and his precepts certainly left no foothold, niche or corner for even the shyest and least conspicuous gnome.

LEFT
Even gnomes in Victorian times indulged in the general trend for taking snuff

RIGHT
Pixieland's aristocratic Lady Joan would no doubt feel at home at Friar Park or Lamport Hall

EACH TO HER OWN

The last word on the subject was spoken, or rather not spoken, by the great Gertrude Jekyll (1843–1942), the major British authority on garden design in the 20th century, who published a magisterial book, entitled simply *Garden Ornament,* in 1918.

There is no mention of gnomes, or even rockeries, in her ruminations on garden statues, urns and vases, bridges and fountains, steps, balustrades, orangeries and loggias, dovecotes, garden seats, pergolas and parterres. Sundials are approved, but Miss Jekyll had misgivings about Italian-style ornament, as not suitable to the English scene. 'The busts of the Caesars and other ornaments and sculptures in white marble are not quite at home in our gardens,' she wrote, and she much preferred statues made of lead. She was very doubtful about topiary work, which she grudgingly admitted could give a garden 'a rare charm, though it is a charm of a whimsical and freakish character.'

Miss Jekyll and the Chelsea Flower Show notwithstanding, gnomes have flourished in suburban, bungalow and occasional cottage gardens ever since the 1920s, though never given more than a contemptuous or joky, superior nod from garden designers, journalists and the gardening magazines. They often appeal especially to elderly and retired couples, perhaps as a substitute for children who have left the nest, or even as trouble-free substitutes for pets, not needing to be fed, exercised or cleaned up after. They appeal to the child behind the adult mask, and there is often a feeling that they bring the household luck and ward off misfortune. But even more fundamentally, gnomes symbolise certain valued qualities, attitudes and aspects of life. They bring into the garden, and so into their owners' hearts and psyches, an air of cheerful unpretentiousness and unaffected good-nature.

LITTLE-GNOME FACT

Gnomes were beneath notice altogether, evidently too whimsical and freakish to be referred to at all. Accordingly, the prestigious Chelsea Flower Show put a ban on 'highly coloured figures, gnomes, fairies, or any similar creatures, actual or mythical, for use as garden ornaments'.

ABOVE
Friendly faces surround Ann Atkin, founder of the Gnome Reserve

A CLASSLESS SOCIETY

Gnomes are given to gardening and fishing, classless pursuits which are two of the most popular pastimes in the country. They are not social climbers. There is nothing snooty about them, they do not give themselves airs and they stimulate lots of affectionate puns ('East, West, Gnome's Best', and so on). They are a statement of what kind of people their owners are, and what kind they want to be, and their gardens are as much an assertion of an ideal as the gardens of Roman antiquity.

Often gnomes are felt to represent closeness to nature and the earth, rejection of society's greed and destructiveness, and concern for the environment. Ann Atkin, for example, who founded the Gnome Reserve in 1979 (see page 96), thinks of them as symbols of a force which lies deep in the universe at large, and also deep in human nature. The typical gnome's hat, she points out, is shaped like a mountain and the 'gnome' inside each human being is a link at an unconscious level of the mind with 'the green', the natural world. A gnome on everyone's desk or workbench, she says, would unconsciously but effectively stimulate awareness of the importance of halting damage to the ecology. In Germany and elsewhere, too, since the 1980s the garden gnome has increasingly been seen in similar terms, as a symbol of the need to protect the environment.

A Gnome-owner's Guide

The English term garden gnome, as we have seen, is a misgnomer, based on a mistranslation of the German *gnomen-figuren* or 'miniature figures' as figures of gnomes. Indeed, German manufacturers call their products garden dwarfs or garden figures, not gnomes.

THE GROWTH OF THE GNOME

THE GERMANS HAVE ALWAYS held a pre-eminent position in the manufacture of these diminutive figures, though a flourishing Far Eastern gnome industry has developed since World War II. In the mid-1990s Germany alone was estimated to be exporting a veritable army of around a million garden figures a year to the rest of the no-doubt unsuspecting world.

LEFT & RIGHT
Early garden figures were remarkably lifelike, whereas this more modern version (right) lacks much of the realism of the original, becoming more stylised

ABOVE RIGHT
This sturdy-looking fellow, now living in Reading, Berkshire, could be a descendant of the orignal Polish gnomes who made their way across Europe

A THRIVING INDUSTRY

In 1994 a minor gnome war smouldered into flame when an infiltration force of 300 Polish-made garden gnomes was detected attempting to cross the German border at Frankfurt an der Oder and seized by customs officials – ignominiously. German manufacturers had been protesting about the invasion of their domestic market by thousands of cheap plaster Polish gnomes, many of them claimed to be pirated copies of German originals. Similarly, in April 1997 it was reported that some 11,000 garden gnomes were again seized by customs officials, this time for illegally travelling through Belgium in an attempt to evade duty. Meanwhile, selling thousands of cheap gnomes to tourists was reported to be playing a useful role in the burgeoning capitalist economy of the new Czech Republic. The gnomes were mostly imported from Thailand, though a few were made by enterprising Czechs in garden workshops. Czechs themselves were said to be not wildly keen on gnomes.

From Saints to Gnomes

One traditional centre of the German industry was the district round Coburg in Bavaria, north of Nuremberg (Prince Albert, Queen Victoria's consort, came from the ducal house of Saxe-Coburg). The area was well known for producing figures of saints and the Holy Family in plaster and terracotta, and when they were not busy with plaster saints, the same artists and craftsmen turned their skills to fashioning gnomes. They were made of local clays mixed in a silo and turned into a liquid paste, which was then run through pipes into the moulds and baked at an extremely high temperature. The figures' arms and hands, the various implements they might be holding, and their big feet in clumping footgear were all made separately of clay and attached later. They were painted individually by hand in the accepted, conventional colours by women, who mostly worked at home.

A Plastic Revolution

After World War II came the invasion of plastic gnomes, made of molten PVC (polyvinyl chloride) poured into metal moulds in similar fashion. After baking in the furnace the moulds are cooled in a water bath and each new-born gnome is summarily yanked out of his mould with a hook which goes through a hole in the base. The figure is then left to cool down further before his clothes, pointed cap and subsequently his face are spray-painted on. The advantage here is that plastic gnomes are hollow and light enough to be easily transported and exported. The hole in the base comes in handy in the garden later, as you can fit your gnome over a peg or a cane pushed into the ground, to prevent him being accidentally knocked over or getting blown down in the wind. Alternatively, the figure's base can be filled with grit or sand to give it greater stability.

Left
This terracotta figure is presumed to originate in Thüringen in about 1950

Below
A PVC Zeho gnome typical of the company

ABOVE & RIGHT
At one time gnomes like these might have been made of lead

GNOMES FOR ALL SEASONS

Many of today's gnomes are made of concrete or synthetic stone, painted in bright colours or given a stone finish. Painted gnomes outdoors tend to suffer from weathering which makes their colours gradually fade over time. To what extent they are likely to be damaged by the effects of frost cracking their paint is a matter of some debate – some manufacturers dismiss the possibility out of hand – but they are often either taken indoors for the winter or wrapped protectively in black plastic sacks. Their owners may playfully describe them as 'hibernating'. Quite a few gnomes end up permanently indoors, where they are safe from the weather and also less at risk of vandalism and theft.

Gnomes are very much an impulse buy. People spot one at a garden centre or shop , take a fancy to him and carry him off home. Gnomes fit into the marketing profile of a successful garden ornament in being easily portable and – most of them, anyway – not impossibly expensive, and they form part of a substantial business. Gardening is one of the most popular pursuits among all classes, and the British

RIGHT & BELOW
Examples of unpainted and painted concrete and synthetic-stone gnomes – familiar sights in millions of gardens

LITTLE-GNOME FACT
The collection at the Gnome Reserve in North Devon includes little lead gnomes which were made in England by Britain's, a company much better known as manufacturers of lead toy soldiers.

alone are said to spend around £80 million a year on garden ornaments. One important factor in their appeal is that they are an instant, almost effortless way to create character and atmosphere in a garden, enabling the owner to put his or her own stamp on it quickly. This helps to account for the popularity of gnomes and other garden ornaments in the 1920s and 1930s, when miles of new ribbon-development suburban housing spread along the roads outside towns, and thousands of families acquired gardens of their own, to make their own. The bandwagon has been kept rolling more recently by a steady increase in the proportion of owner-occupiers in the population. The water garden sector has also developed rapidly for the same reason.

LEFT & BELOW
Some of the most colourful figures can be found among the water gardens (or near by) enjoying a spot of fishing

KNOW YOUR GNOME

SPECIAL FEATURES & SUBTLE DIFFERENCES

Gnomes come in a wide range of sizes and hundreds of different types. Most range in height from about 4–18 inches (10–45cm), but there are taller ones, with monster specimens standing as high as 3ft 3in (1m). One of the leading manufacturesr of plastic figures, Zeho of Coburg in Germany, exports massive 1-metre gnomes which have white beards and side-whiskers and locks of white hair falling from under their bright red pointed caps. They wear jackets of red, blue, green or yellow; and red, green or yellow trousers, fastened with a leather belt or tied round with string. They have heavy boots, in some cases with holes through which a toe is peeping. One of them is pushing a wooden wheelbarrow, while others may be holding a lamp, a rake or a pipe. They have bright blue or brown eyes, turned-up noses, broad grins, gleaming white teeth and determinedly cheery expressions, and they are all looking trustingly upwards – at their owners.

LEFT
A rather portly figure from the Garden Dwarf Museum

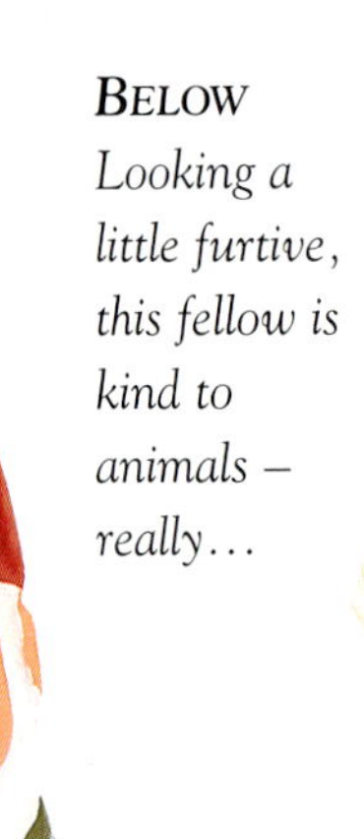

BELOW
Looking a little furtive, this fellow is kind to animals – really…

BELOW
There seems to be no limit to items carried or collected by gnomes, including a wide variety of flora and fauna

LITTLE-GNOME FACT
A magnificent lifesize gnome gazes out at the world from the second floor of Liberty's in London's Regent Street.

BELOW
These tiny acrobatic tumblers make fun cake decorations

LEFT
Not a lot of people know that gnomes from Australia are noted for their green hats

RIGHT
Relative size or scale doesn't really matter in the fantasy world of gnomes and their surroundings

ABOVE
He may be bare foot, but this Canadian chap is clearly happy with just his music

RIGHT
Studious-looking 'Big George' may seem strong and sturdy, but his 20-in (51cm) ceramic frame is really quite fragile

Gnomes Galore

The Zeho company of Coburg, Germany produces an impressive array of gnomes and other garden figures, designed to reflect the interests of their owners. Figures may be holding a pickaxe, a spade or a scythe, or pushing a wheelbarrow or clutching an outsize fish almost as big as the gnome himself.

Some of the gnomes are much given to music and play a variety of instruments, from squeeze-box to guitar, violin, trumpet, saxophone, double-bass and drums, and one even has an alpenhorn. One figure is going shooting in knickerbockers and a feathered hat, clutching a pair of binoculars and with his gun slung on his back. Another is sitting quietly reading a book, his spectacles pushed up on his forehead, and one is simply standing with his hands in his pocket, gazing thoughtfully into space. One (known in the trade as Smiler) is seated bare-bottomed on a chamber pot. Another is holding a house plant and one with a rather impenetrable look on his face is waving goodbye, or could it be hello?

Above
Like his friends the gnomes, this little leprechaun enjoys nothing more than striking up a tune

Left
Chopping wood may be a thing of the past for most people, but many gnomes still carry axes

Right
This is a very useful chappie to have around, as he comes with his own plant holder, ideal for indoors or out

NEVER EMPTY-HANDED

Angling gnomes are a very popular model, dressed traditionally in waders, fishing up an old boot from the pond. Typically, gnomes may be shown busy at their gardening tasks, wielding barrows, saws, axes, spades, watering cans or other tools of the trade. Pipe-smoking is another popular trend, while others carry cups, mugs and other drinking vessels, and have been known be so far gone in drink that they need to clutch a lamp-post for support.

Some gnomes like to proudly display the fruits of their gardening labours – or perhaps those of their owners. They have picked a bunch of flowers or they are holding up a cauliflower or a cabbage or they have just planted a small tree. One or two of them are displaying the fruits of other labours – fondly cradling a gnome baby or carrying one on their backs. Others like to show their solidarity with animal life by cradlng a small bird or a squirrel or petting a bambi-style deer, and, perhaps strangely, riding piggyback is a popular pastime. There are also various spotted toadstools and a toadstool house which stands a little over 1ft (32cm) high, as well as figures of deer, squirrels, foxes, rabbits, dogs and cats, snails, hedgehogs, tortoises, ducks and chickens, dolphins and small children.

BELOW
Gnomes have an affinity with all manner of plants and animals

LEFT
One of the hundreds of Zeho plastic gnomes, making use of a novel form of transport

Klein aber
mein

Unusual Variations

Another German manufacturer, Gustav Liebermann of Neustadt bei Coburg (previously Max Denner, founded in 1918) makes a similar range of plastic gnomes and animal figures, which are cheaper and less detailed. Some of their gnomes poses are more unusual, for example one is freshening up the paint job on a toadstool, and another is sunbathing on a chaise longue wearing sunglasses and smoking a stumpy cigar in tycoon fashion. A nautical gnome is steering a ship and there is a plump, demure female gnome in a blue dress and a pearl necklace.

Zeho-style plastic gnomes and other garden ornaments are made in Austria by the Hofmann firm at Grossraming in the romantic Enns valley, in the Alps. It turns out 250,000 gnomes a year, some 80 per cent of whom emigrate to spend their lives in the USA, Switzerland, France and Japan. 'There is so much murder and killing in the world,' Ulrich Hofmann says, 'perhaps this is why the friendly, harmless garden dwarfs are so popular.' His company makes about 250 different types, adding a few new ones each year. The company will manufacture custom-designed gnomes on request, though they are naturally expensive, and customers in Austria quite often ask for gnomes which look like one of their neighbours.

Left
Gnomes are sociable creatures, and enjoy relaxing round toadstools

LITTLE-GNOME FACT

There are reckoned to be well over one million gnomes resident in Austrian gardens, window-boxes, homes and offices, with the gnome population rising steadily, though the same yawning gulf between those who love gnomes and those who detest them as sentimental kitsch exists on mainland Europe as in Britain.

Right
The popularity of hardwearing, washable plastic figures is evident from the huge variety made and exported around the world

HAPPY SMILING FACES

YOU CAN SEE IT IN THEIR EYES

The expressions on the faces of gnomes makes a study in itself. Many of them are smiling merrily, and most of them, whether smiling or not, look healthily cheerful. It is their happy, trusting faces that people like so much, and by looking happy they help to create happiness around them. Some gnomes, however, have a thoughtful and reflective aspect, some look really rather bad-tempered and a few are mildly tiddly, if not totally inebriated. Some look startled, as if they have been suddenly taken by surprise, and a few look as if they are not quite right in the head. The sanity of the occasional rogue garden gnome seems distinctly questionable.

LEFT
This little pointing gnome has such a cheery face that not even the most hard-hearted motorist could resist offering him a lift in his travels

ABOVE
The slightly glazed expression is only natural after a drop of cider

RIGHT
This chap is just full of bare-faced cheek

RIGHT
This fellow looks somewhat startled, and even a little shy

Below
As with humans, the wearing of glasses imparts an intelligent look to already lifelike features

Above
The eyes here look a little sinister, an impression enhanced by the axe

Above
A youngster showing wide-eyed innocence

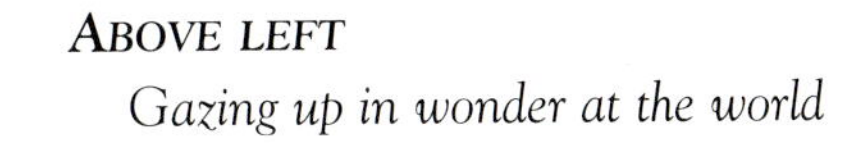

Above left
Gazing up in wonder at the world

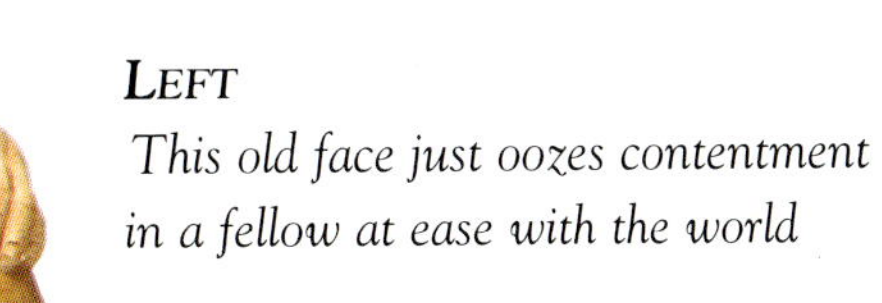

Left
This old face just oozes contentment in a fellow at ease with the world

Below
This chap has a rather crafty or sneaky look about him – perhaps an expert at the game, or maybe he's up to something a little underhand

Made in Britain

Based in Birmingham and at Blackburn in Lancashire, Silver Lynx Products import 10,000 or so gnomes into the United Kingdom from China every year, along with other garden ornaments. The brand name is Artline and the gnomes are made of plastic resin, on to which the colours are bonded, as a protection against fading through exposure to the weather. They include gardening and fishing gnomes, and gnomes with musical instruments, as well as a popular leprechaun and figures of animals, birds and small children, windmills, weathervanes, whirlygigs, bird baths and other garden ornaments.

Below
One in a series of wide-eyed old men in the Silver Lynx range of figures

Above
Hundreds of unpainted concrete gnomes, pixies and other figures stand like China's terracotta warriors at Whelan's in Sheerness

The United Kingdom's largest manufacturers of concrete garden ornaments, including numerous gnomes, are Whelan's of Sheerness in Kent. They make classical-style urns and planters, troughs and bird baths, sundials and figures of animals, shapely nymphs, playful cherubs and sentimentalised children, as well as cricketers, a Snow White figure with seven dwarfs and two elves on a seesaw. Most of their gnomes are doing the usual accepted gnome-type activities – pushing wheelbarrows, wielding watering cans, playing musical instruments, reading books, holding vegetables, cradling small animals. One of the figures is idly lying on his stomach, supporting his head on his hand. A blacksmith model works at his anvil, while there are car drivers and riders aboard a grinning snail.

RIGHT
A visitor from Germany, but clearly enjoying motoring around Britain

RIGHT
Shameless is the only way to describe some of the new generation of gnomes at the Garden Dwarf Museum in Rot am See, Germany

RIGHT
This cheeky chappie is surely old enough to know better

GNOMES BEHAVING BADLY

Gnomes are not always as innocent as they seem, and quite a few figures are decidedly smutty. Whelan's make a rather well-endowed 'flasher' gnome and one with a severe case of builder's cleavage, while another has pushed his trousers right down and is derisively 'mooning'

LEFT
This buxom wench has probably seen better days

Left
Blatant exhibitionism, or just another reflection of falling standards in modern society?

the onlookers with his bare backside and looking round over his shoulder to judge the effect.

This may be a distant reminiscence of the Egyptian dwarf god Bes putting his tongue out to drive away evil spirits and bad luck, and perhaps a return to the ugly, grotesque 18th-century German garden dwarfs, but is out of kilter with the traditional brownie's concern to keep up standards and punish sluttishness.

The suggestive, rude or crudely sexual figure seems to be a fairly recent addition to the gnome population, for although garden gnomes have been fiercely criticised in the past for their sentimentality, one of their attractive qualities was always their cheerful and friendly innocence. However, judging from the wide range of 'vulgar' gnomes available, they obviously have a place in modern society.

People make their gardens in their own image, to create a harmony which expresses their idea of themselves, their values and their aspirations. The variety of gnomes and the activities which define their characters appeal to different garden-owners' pictures of their ideal selves and their idyllic life – whether spent fishing or gardening or playing music or drinking or idling or in some anxiety-free combination of activities.

Below
A decidedly bijou residence, but ideal for the single gnome

Size Doesn't Matter

Questions of relative scale seldom seem to affect these utopian scenes and people often mix figures of different sizes and types together with no feeling of incongruity. Gnomes and their friends can be much too big for their associated Swiss chalet or working windmill, for instance, without it worrying anyone.

Toadstools can be gnomes' tables or shelters for gnomes to keep out of the rain beneath or houses for gnomes to live in, complete with windows and a little stovepipe chimney sticking out of the roof, and sometimes a gnome or two peeping out through a window. How big the toadstool is and how big the gnomes are does not really seem to matter. This is a fantasy world, after all.

Magic Mushrooms

Mushrooms and toadstools have been closely associated with the little people since at least the 17th century. Their mysteriously sudden appearance from underground and their miraculously

Above
Bright colours make mushrooms and toad-stools attractive, but sometimes dangerous

LITTLE-GNOME FACT

The libretto of Humperdinck's 1893 opera *Hänsel und Gretel* includes a riddle about the identity of a diminutive 'manling', who stands quite still on one leg in the forest all day, wearing a purple mantle: the answer is a mushroom.

swift burgeoning, combined with the odd shapes and striking colours of toadstools – some of which glow in the dark – gave them an uncanny reputation in folk tradition. This was reinforced by the fact that some of them are poisonous or have hallucinogenic effects – traits that rather belie their fanciful names. The link with fairyland is conveyed in mushrooms and toadstools called Fairy Cake, Fairies Bonnets, Slender Elf Cap and Dune Pixie Hood. Fairy Ring Champignons form the boundaries of fairy rings and there are also fungi called Fairy Club and Elfin's Saddle.

It's a Man's World

Almost all garden gnomes are adult males: female ones, children and gnome families appear less often, and when they do it is more frequently at tourist attractions or in fantasy books than in gardens. In the oldest northern European traditions dwarfs are an exclusively male race. As they live for ever, they have no need to reproduce their species, and thus no need of females.

Dwarfs of later traditions may not have enjoyed eternal life, but they lived for centuries, and no one seems to have worried about how they would keep their numbers up. Male gnomes are seldom young; they are almost always vigorously hale and hearty, certainly, but their white hair and beards would indicate that they are no longer in the first flush of their manhood, so perhaps they have no need of better halves, or perhaps they keep their womenfolk out of sight.

The rare word 'gnomide' is recorded in the 18th century for a female earth elemental of the Paracelsus type, but there is no real tradition of gnome femininity and a campaign in Germany by *Bild* newspaper in 1962 to create a generally acceptable female gnome was a flop.

Right
The fair 'Demelza', from Gnome World

Above
A delicate terracotta 'gnomette', made by Heissner in about 1960

Below
Mushrooms at the Gnome Reserve provide ideal resting places for a pair of tiny musicians

Workers and Shirkers

Handy Helpers or Lazy Good-for-nothings?

Over the last 200 years or so, the garden gnome has come to be a colourful feature of millions of gardens worldwide. His attire and expression may vary, but he is usually a willing worker, busying himself with various tasks around the home and garden. However, as with humans, there are always exceptions to the rule – skivers and shirkers among the hard workers.

Left
This wide-eyed youngster is far too engrossed in his book to bother with anything as strenuous as work

Above
This modern blacksmith is obviously happy in his work

Below
Wheelbarrow at the ready, this chap is a great help clearing up around the garden

Right
A spot of fishing – a garden gnome's favourite hobby

Far right
Very much a human trait – loitering with intent to do nothing at all

Left
Smithying and forging has been a traditional activity from the very earliest days of garden figures

Below
Keeping the lawns in trim is hard work

Left
Pipe-smoking is allowed, but only after a hard day's labour

Above
Why work when you can spend the day dozing beside a toadstool?

WORK...

Although some gnomes stand or loll about doing little or nothing, most are occupied in one way or another or are at least making some decent pretence of activity. Their main occupations are gardening or fishing. Some are connected to watering cans or hosepipes so that they actually do water the garden. Although there is a strong strain of mine-spirit in their ancestry, and the odd gnome can be seen holding a bag of gold, very few gnomes nowadays are engaged in mining or any kind of industrial activity. This helps their owners to think of them as 'green' and environmentally conscientious beings. You may see a gnome postman once in a while, but attempts to link them with human jobs generally fail, as they clash with the gardener's ambition to create an ideal world, separate from the humdrum sphere of routine work.

...REST

Gnomes are constantly represented as kind to animals and even when one is clutching a huge fish, he is of course going

LEFT
This shepherd obviously likes to keep a very close watch over his flock

BELOW
The squeeze-box is popular even amongst Bavarian figures like this 1950s' model

BELOW
These two instrumentalists have been making music since the 1940s

to put it back in the water as soon as he has finished showing it off. The musical activities of gnomes also imply harmony and a certain high-mindedness, and there are hiking and climbing gnomes who enjoy socially approved country pursuits. The occasional gnome holds an old-style storm lantern, as if to welcome you home or help you in the dark (a cynic would wonder if he is secretly hoping, like a pixie or a will-o-the-wisp, to lead you astray for a laugh).

LEFT
Hiking is one of the more energetic pursuits, undertaken by a few hardy gnomes

ABOVE
Political gatherings never used to be as colourful as this

...AND PLAY

Gnomes are sometimes shown playing cards with a toadstool as a handy table, the occasional Scottish one may be seen dancing a reel in a kilt – though gnomes are not very popular in Scotland, where they tend to be classed with other English invaders – and others enjoy nothing better than swinging on a branch of ivy, a trailing plant or a wooden garden swing.

FAMOUS FACES

Perhaps surprisingly, celebrity gnomes do not sell particularly well, maybe because they bring the real, everyday world unwantedly close. Following the first successful landing on the moon in 1969, the German newspaper *Bild* ordered a consignment of astronaut gnomes equipped with helmets, pickaxes and moon rock, but few readers wanted to buy them. Nor have many gardeners in Europe warmed to gnomes made in the image of Konrad Adenauer or Helmut Kohl, General de Gaulle or President John F Kennedy, while Margaret Thatcher gnomes and John Major gnomes have made comparatively little impact in Britain.

FROM HUMBLE BEGINNINGS...

John Major is associated with gnomes in another way, through his family business. The former British Prime Minister's father, who started life as Abraham Thomas Ball in 1879, adopted Major as his stage name. After spending most of his childhood in America and returning to Walsall with his parents, he ran away to join a circus as a clown and acrobat, and spent many years as a variety artiste, singing, dancing and doing comic sketches and conjuring tricks. He retired in his early fifties and settled down with his young second wife to run a garden ornaments business from their home in Longfellow Road, among the amiable suburban bungalows of Worcester Park in the south-west of London. He chose his moment well, for the area was being developed, with new suburban homes going up close by in Ewell and Stoneleigh, equipped with brand-new gardens whose proud owners were keen to put their stamp on them.

The business prospered and Tom Major opened a workshop in Surbiton as well as the one at home in Longfellow Road. His gnomes were resplendent in red caps, green coats and brown trousers, and had grey beards flecked in black and white. Besides gnomes he made statues of nymphs and figures of animals including hedgehogs, squirrels, ducks, frogs, dogs, rabbits and herons, making the original moulds himself. He also sold bird baths, tubs for shrubs, turf and crazy paving, and supplied ornaments to substantial retailers in the area, including the big Bentall's department store in Kingston upon Thames.

The war knocked the business on the head as demand for garden ornaments collapsed. Digging might be needed for victory, but gnomes were not credited with a key role in defeating Hitler. Tom Major restarted the firm after 1945 and opened a workshop near Worcester Park station, but he was getting old and finances were difficult. The family moved to Coldharbour Lane in Brixton in 1955 and Terry Major-Ball, the elder son, continued the garden ornament trade as best he could from a workshop in Camberwell. New capital came in when Major's Garden Ornaments was bought in 1959 by a Commander David of David's Rural Industries, who employed Terry to work for him, making cement ornaments and bird baths with a veneer of marble or Portland Stone. The youthful John Major worked in the business for a year or two, before setting off on the path that would eventually take him to 10 Downing Street. Meanwhile, Tom Major died in 1962. Although he made and sold hundreds of gnomes in his time, very few can be identified today.

BELOW
Hard at work in the garden of Terry Major-Ball, John Major's brother

LEFT
Stone garden figures were the making of the Major family business

WORTHLESS KITSCH?

Viewed as antiques and collectors' items, it has to be admitted that gnomes are small beer. Though of great sentimental value to their loving owners, they are worth relatively little money. The amount of enthusiasm that even the older and more distinguished ceramic gnomes arouse in the leading auction houses would scarcely fill an undernourished acorn, but there are a few exceptions to the rule.

The Lamport Hall gnome, sole survivor of Sir Charles Isham's brood, may have been insured for £1 million, but that was for publicity purposes, and it would not fetch anything approaching that figure at auction. However, a set of ten 18th-century sandstone gnomes has been valued at some £5,000–6,500 by *Miller's Guide*, and others are listed in the high hundreds, including the figure holding a hare and the Victorian brass gnome with umbrella on page 37, at £750–1,500 and £500–600 respectively.

Christie's is said to have sold a group of ten gnomes for £1,650 in 1989, and at Sotheby's, more recently, a German specimen dated to about 1910, smoking a meerschaum pipe and holding a garden rake, was given an estimate of between £200 to £400 and sold towards the higher end of that range.

Christie's is no longer interested in garden gnomes, and James Rylands, who heads the garden statuary and furniture department of Sotheby's, does not want gnomes in his auctions, which he feels would be trivialised and devalued by their presence. Quite separately, however, he has an appreciative recollection of a gnomish pun he encountered in the mid-1980s at a gnome show at Longleat, Wiltshire, where some bandaged and apparently sick gnomes were arranged in a mock hospital ward under a banner reading 'National Elf Service'.

ABOVE
In 1997 this gnome on a garden swing, dated between 1900 and 1920, was valued at £500 by Judith Miller of Miller's Guide; *left, another example of the genre from* Miller's

VALUED POSSESSIONS

Some of the more valuable examples of garden figures are, as would be expected, the antique variety from the earlier manufacturers, some which have already appeared elsewhere. Notable among these are the porcelain models of the type made by the Heissner company at Gräfenroda and by Ludwig Möller near by in Erfurt, Germany. The figures were extremely striking and expressed great character. Many were seen in traditional poses, carrying out the usual activities or indulging in typical country pursuits such as hunting.

LEFT & ABOVE RIGHT
Typical examples from a 19th-century advertisement for the Ludwig Möller range of garden ornaments

ABOVE
The Heissner catalogue contained a wide range of garden dwarfs and other figures

A GNOME OF ONE'S OWN

WHY SETTLE FOR ANY common or garden gnome when you could be the envy of your fellow gnome-owners with your very own, custom-made model? With a little imagination and few inhibitions, the results can be quite surprising.

Here's One We Made Earlier

Using a latex mould and household items, it is rewarding to make your own gnome, which you can decorate in a number of ways, experimenting with different effects for indoor and outdoor use. It is important to work in a well-ventilated area on the floor, as heavy weights are involved. Indeed, an extra pair of hands may be needed for some stages. Warm conditions will help speed up drying processes. Use a barrier cream or wear gloves to protect the hands. This is a messy process, so have some water to hand and plenty of newspaper. It is always a good idea to read through all the relevant instructions first, so that you are fully prepared before starting.

YOU WILL NEED

Latex mould (assorted models are available from selected garden gnome suppliers)
Gloves/barrier cream
Soft sand
Sharp sand
Cement
Water (a supply of running water near by is preferable)
Hardboard/MDF/thick card
Wooden battens
Bucket (taller than the latex mould)
Plastic bowls
Washing-up liquid
Craft knife
Jigsaw/coping saw (optional)
Filling/palette knife
PVA sealer and/or polyurethane varnish
Polyfilla/car-body filler (for general repairs)
Paints and assorted brushes
Palette for mixing paints
Sticks
Sponges
Cloths, duster
Garden trowel (optional)
Masking tape
Toothbrush (optional)

1 First make a support for the mould. Soak the mould in water then place the base on a piece of hardboard/thick cardboard/MDF about 3mm (⅛in) thick – enough to support the weight of the mould when filled with the sand/cement mixture. Press down firmly on the base to leave an impression of the shape of the feet (omit this stage if you do not want free-standing feet).

2 Draw round the shape, leaving a few millimetres all round, and cut it out carefully with a jigsaw, coping saw or craft knife.

3 Fill the bucket part-way with sharp sand, leaving a hollow for the mould. Wet the inside of the mould, fit it into the support and suspend it over two battens placed across the rim of the bucket.

4 In a bucket or bowl mix together the sharp sand and cement using a ratio of two parts sand to one part cement. Gradually add water while stirring until the mixture is the consistency of thick cream. Some practice is needed here.

5 The mixture should pour easily: too thick and it will not flow into the crevices of the mould, too thin and the cast will be weak when set. When you are happy with its consistency, pour the cement mixture into the mould.

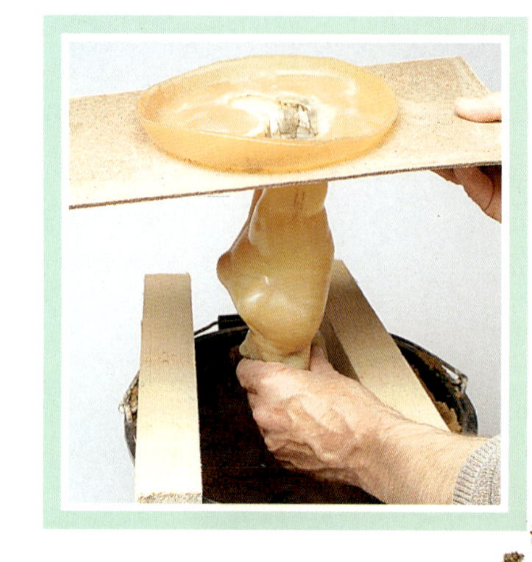

6 Squash and jiggle the mould around to expel air bubbles. Shape more sand around the mould to support it, but take care not to pack it too tightly so as to distort the shape.

7 Keep tapping the mould to avoid air bubbles and poke the mixture with a stick to make sure all bubbles are removed. Fill until flush with the feet unless using the base as a stand. Leave the cast to set in a dry place.

8 When dry, carefully scoop the sand out from around the mould. It may be easier to use your hand initially, then continue with a trowel.

9 Gently lift the mould out of the bucket, supporting the whole thing. Brush away the sand and apply soapy water to the outside of the mould to aid its removal.

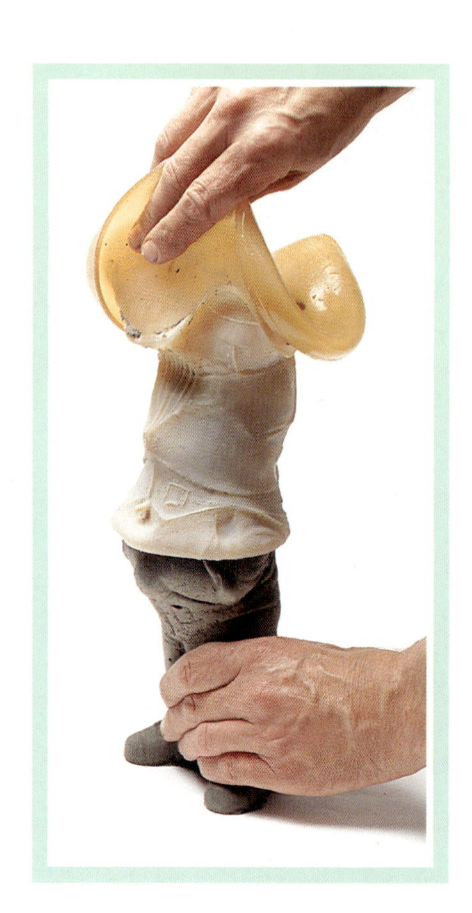

10 Taking care with the slippery latex, gently ease the mould away from the base of the cast. Now carefully, slowly and in one continuous movement pull the mould up off the cast so that it turns inside out. (If the cement is still a little wet the cast could break.)

11 Trim off any excess flanges of cement from around the feet and leave the gnome to dry completely. Meanwhile, rinse the mould thoroughly as traces of soap will damage the latex. Use a sponge or toothbrush to remove any traces of sand/cement.

12 You will no doubt find some air holes and other holes and blemishes. Fill in any largish holes with some polyfilla on a small knife or spatula.

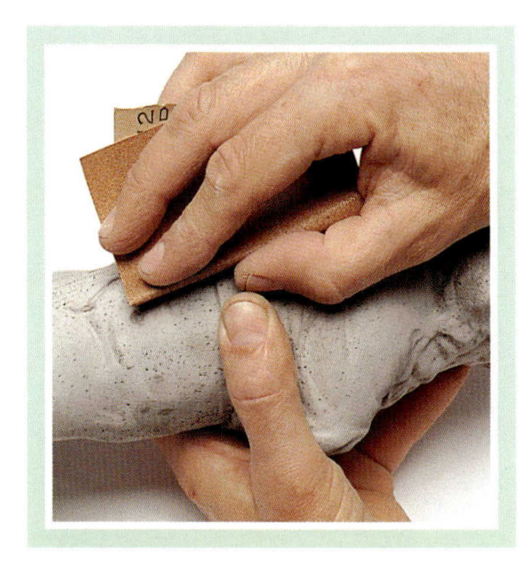

13 Using a piece of glasspaper, sand the cast all over, smoothing down any remaining rough areas.

14 Use some polyfilla on a sponge to penetrate right into any remaining smaller air holes in preparation for decorating the model.

Problem Solving

A If you failed to expel all the air bubbles when filling the mould, or if the mixture was not of the right consistency, holes will appear on the cast. Fill these in using polyfilla applied with a palette knife or spatula.

B Accidents somtimes happen when removing the model from the mould, so take care not to drop it. Here one of the gnome's feet broke off when the latex mould was being removed from the cast.

C To repair the damage, mix up some epoxy glue according to the instructions, apply to the broken parts, and press together firmly. Wipe off any excess glue. Hold the pieces in place with masking tape if necessary, and leave to set.

D When the glue has completely set, fill in any large gaps still remaining with polyfilla. Any medium-sized holes can be smoothed over with some fiiler on a sponge as before.

If using gloss or enamel paints, apply these straight on to the surface to be painted. Alternatively, acrylic paints offer brighter and more varied colours and are easier to mix. They must be diluted with water first.

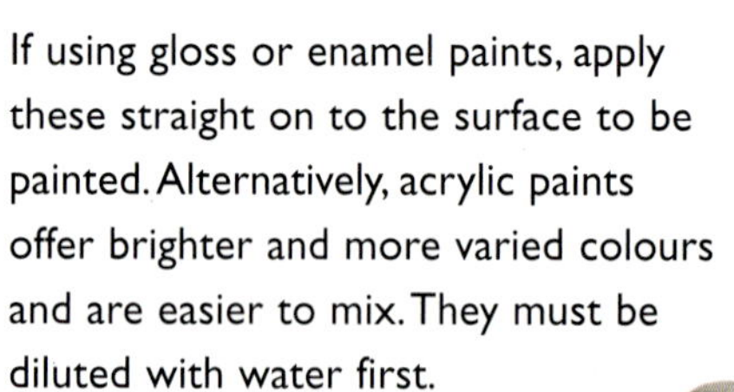

15 Seal the cast all over with PVA or clear varnish before painting, making sure that the undersides of the feet are done. As the gnome will be left outdoors, the painted surfaces must be weatherproof.

16 It may be useful to plan out your colour scheme in advance by making a sketch of the gnome and marking it out as if painting by numbers. Start with the larger areas, leaving each coat to dry before moving on to another area or adding another coat.

17 While waiting for one coat of paint to dry on the bulk of the model, start on the face and features. Aim for a flesh-coloured tone, but this could take some trial and error with mixing if using acrylic paints.

18 Two coats of paint will be sufficient for the larger areas of the body and for the hat. As this is your own gnome, you are not bound by any colour conventions for hats.

19 Fiddly details like the eyes can be left until last. They require a very fine brush and a steady hand.

20 The painting is almost complete now, with just a little tidying up required in places. The lips on this example look a little on the full side, as it is easy to get carried away.

Variations on a Theme

It is amazing how the same model can be made to look completely different just by altering the colour scheme, giving him thinner lips or larger eyes, or by experimenting with different decorative effects.

1 An interesting effect can be obtained by painting the gnome all over with matt black, oil-based paint (blackboard paint).

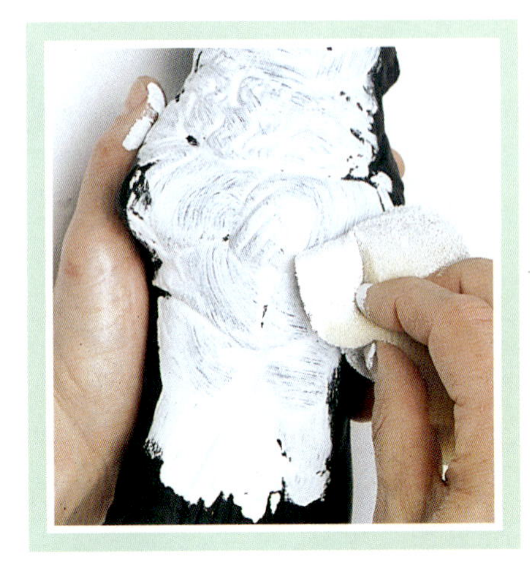

2 When the black layer is dry, use a sponge to rub the model all over with some white masonry paint.

3 Quickly wipe off the residue of the paint to leave the white in all the crevices of the cast. The finished effect is of a silvery gnome, reminiscent of some of the older lead models.

1 Alternatively, try this rather effective-looking ageing technique. Using an old toothbrush to get into all the crevices, coat the cast all over with dark green acrylic paint.

2 While still wet, wipe off the excess paint to leave a verdigris effect in the nooks and crannies, the equivalent of leaving the gnome at the mercy of the elements to gather moss.

1 This is another very effective technique that can be applied to the finished model. After sealing as before with PVA, paint the gnome all over with a couple of coats of gold paint, making sure each coat is completely dry before applying the next.

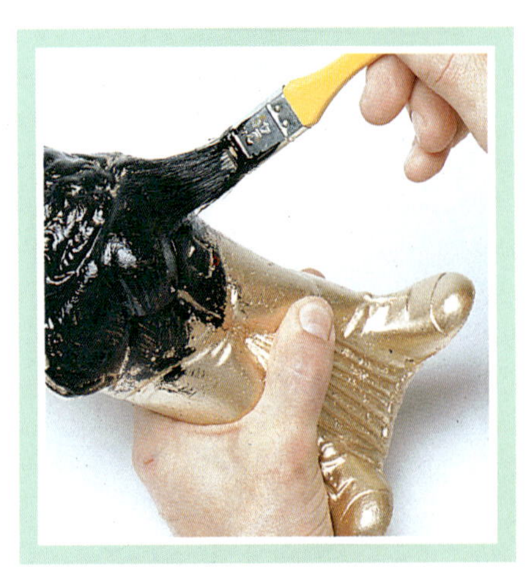

2 When the gold paint is dry, apply two coats of matt black (blackboard) paint to the model, again letting the first coat dry before applying the second coat.

3 While wet, wipe off some of the paint with a sponge, then buff up the surface with a duster to create a gilt finish. Gold highlights can added later if required. This variation is probably best suited for indoors, so there is no need for a final coat of varnish.

1 Here is a prime example of how different the same model can look with just a different colour scheme. The cast has been sealed as before, and this time gloss or enamel paints are applied straight on to the model.

2 Again you can plan out your colour scheme in advance with a marked-out sketch. Don't be afraid to be bold and experiment with very bright colours or unusual combinations, as they can look very effective.

Repairs and Maintenance

Many gnome owners have favourites who, certainly not through neglect, may have seen better days. No-one likes to part with dear friends, so why not have a go at sprucing them up. Here we look at a couple of basic techniques.

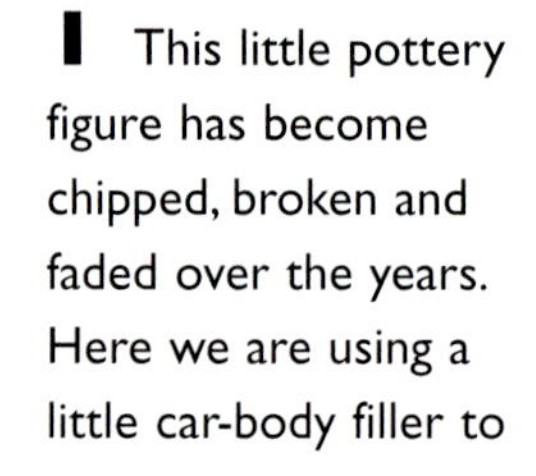

1 This little pottery figure has become chipped, broken and faded over the years. Here we are using a little car-body filler to

2 A little more accuracy is needed when repairing small or awkward features like the broken nose and eroded cheek area.

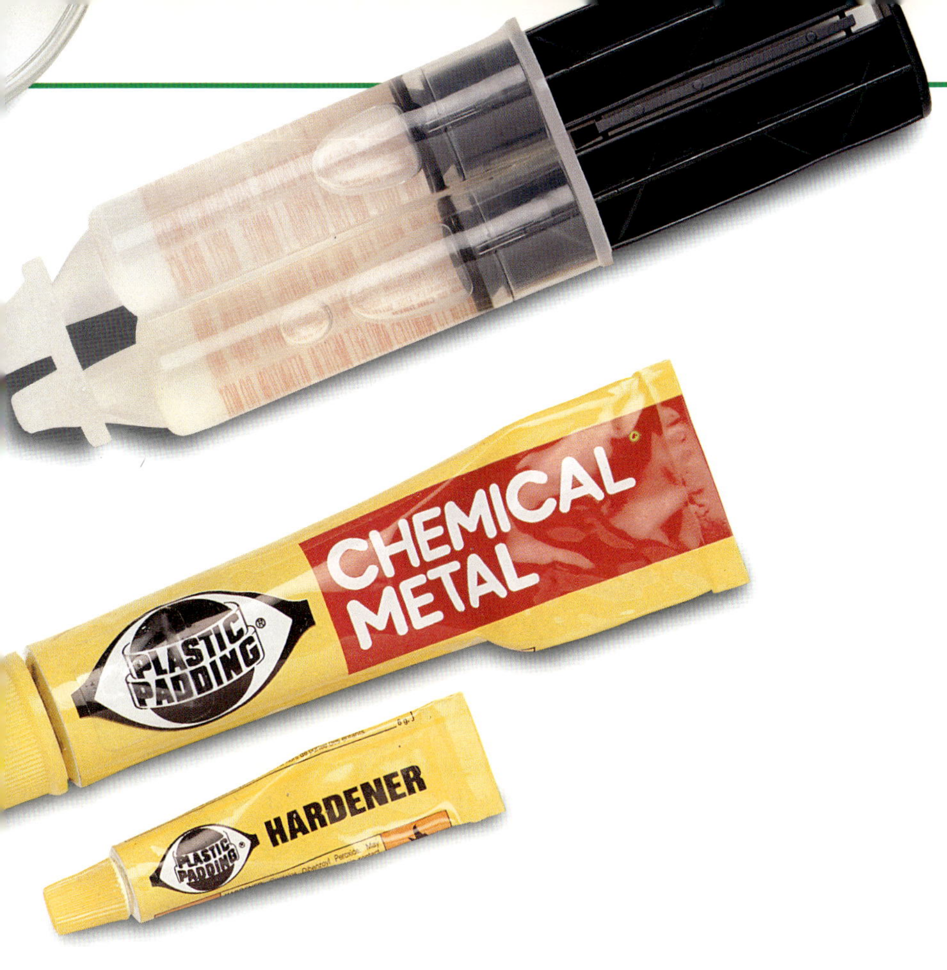

3 It is very easy to use too much filler here, as the area under repair is small and rather fiddly. If you do overdo things, wipe off the excess while still wet, or chip it away if dry.

4 Let the filler set and then sand the repaired areas smooth with some glasspaper, using the corners to reach into awkward areas. Any extra general shaping can also be done at this stage.

5 The repaired areas are now ready for painting. Try to match the original colours as far as possible.

6 If you have trouble matching the original paintwork, or there are large areas to be done, it may be easier to repaint the whole figure. Although perhaps looking a little sheepish about his new 'nose job', our finished gnome looks much perkier and is now good for a few more summers at least.

1 Here we look at a simple repair to an old stone patrol gnome who has fallen over and suffered an unfortunate breakdown.

2 Brush away any loose material and then apply some epoxy glue to the broken surfaces. Press together tightly and quickly wipe off any excess glue.

3&4 Tape the gnome together firmly with masking tape and allow the glue to set. You may need to leave it overnight. When set, carefully remove the tape, roughen the surface to accept the new paint, then finish by retouching, again matching colours as closely as possible.

The Professionals at Work

Following our attempts at making, decorating and repairing our own gnomes, this is a brief look at how the professionals do it, with a glimpse behind the scenes at the production line at the Gartenzwerg Museum (Garden Dwarf Museum) at Rot am See, Germany (see pages 106–8). Garden dwarfs, as we know they are called in Germany and elsewhere, are big business, but the process of making the gnomes still retains some personal touches, despite the sheer numbers involved. The finished 'cowboy' gnome (or should that be 'pigboy'?) is a gleaming example of the wide range of figures produced here.

2 A clay mould is also made of the pig, which, as we have seen elsewhere, is a very popular mode of transport among garden gnomes.

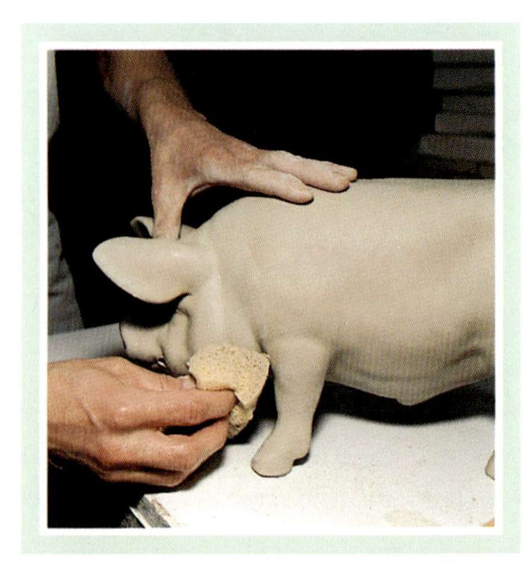

3 Both the figure and the pig are then smoothed over with a damp sponge to get rid of any blemishes.

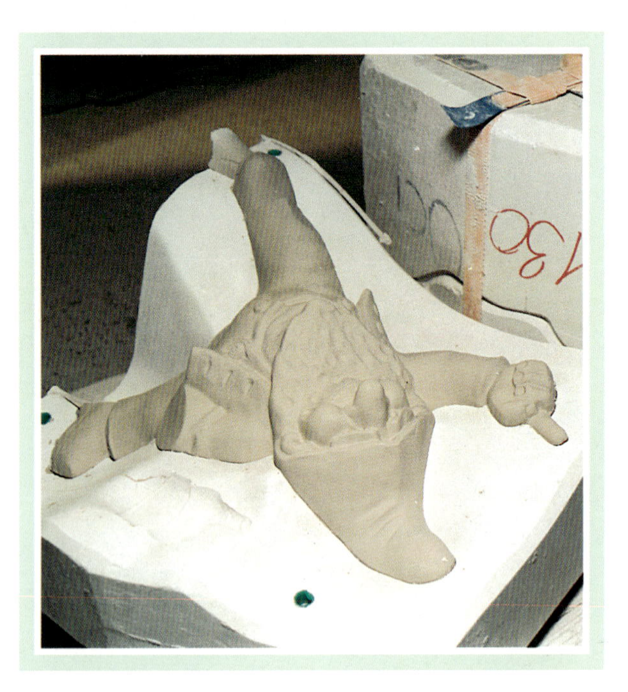

1 Instead of concrete or stone, these examples are modelled in clay. The liquid clay is poured into split moulds and left to harden, after which the mould is taken apart carefully to reveal the cast of the figure.

4 The dwarf and his pig are now joined together firmly and the joins smoothed over. Both parts are then fired in the kiln.

5 After firing, the figures are lovingly hand painted in bright colours by dedicated employees (almost exclusively women) either at the factory or working from home.

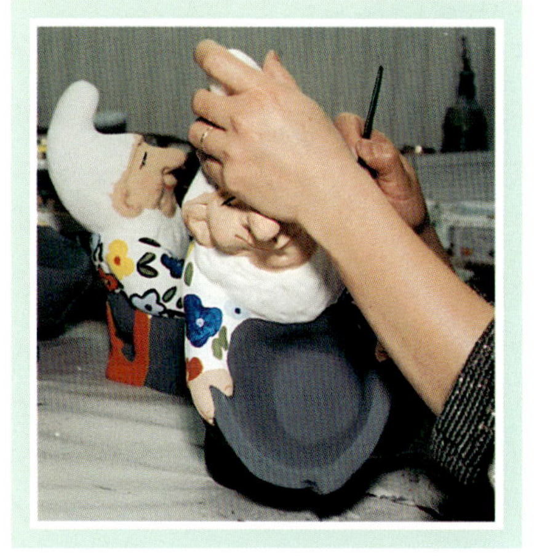

6 Here another figure in the range made by the factory receives similar treatment, and some finishing touches are added before the gnomes are ready to leave for their new homes and gardens.

7 The final stage is to give the figures a hardwearing coat of varnish to protect them from the elements. As we have seen, standing out in the garden each summer year after year can take its toll.

SAFE AND SECURE

Having bought or, better still, made some gnomes, anxious gnome owners tend to position their little people in the back garden rather than the front, and at points where an eye can be kept on them, for fear of theft or vandalism. Like so many things associated with gnomes, insuring them is not entirely a simple matter. The big insurance companies generally include garden gnomes automatically in their ordinary house and contents policies. The gnomes are covered within a stated maximum amount (£500 or some such figure) for the entire garden contents. However, you will probably have to bear the first £50 or so of each loss yourself, and most gnomes are going to be worth less than that. If you own one or more expensive gnomes and they and your other garden contents are worth more than the stated maximum, it is worth paying a bit extra for adequate coverage. However, the gnomes are only covered when on your own home ground. If you take one walkabout, you are not protected.

The policy will cover you against theft and vandalism, and if something falls on your poor gnome from a great height – a tree or a branch, a lamp post or telegraph pole, or something dropped from a passing aeroplane – the damage should be covered. So is damage caused by lightning, flood, fire, smoke, subsidence and earthquake. You need to find out whether accidental breakage is covered by the policy or not. Malicious damage caused by anyone who is lawfully on your property may be ruled out, and so may any damage caused by pets. Insurance companies do not cover gnomes against damage by frost, weathering and ordinary natural wear and tear.

If you have valuable gnomes to insure, the best bet is probably to get an insurance broking firm to arrange it for you. This will not increase the premium you pay, as the broker's commission is paid by the company. Alternatively, you can deal direct with one of the large, well-known companies that already insure most people's homes and cars, though a professional will know more of the right questions to ask and may well get you a more satisfactory deal – which, like all insurance, is not necessarily the same as the cheapest deal when it comes to claim time.

LITTLE-GNOME FACT

According to reports from the USA, the latest technology has turned the gnome-crime situation upside down, with gnomes linked to surveillance cameras now actually helping to guard the home against crime. This is a striking rediscovery of the household spirit's traditional role as guardian of the household against evil and misfortune. They can also be fitted with recorded messages so that, for instance, when you turn up as a guest at someone's house, the attendant gnome can tell you that the family are having a barbecue and to go round to the garden.

The Gnoming Instinct

One of the major attractions of gnomes is their ability to inspire fantasies – appealing to the buried childishness in adults, encouraging its rediscovery and release.

THE REALMS OF FANTASY

ALAN QUARTERMAN has been making concrete garden gnomes at Gnome World, at Indian Queens in Cornwall, since the early 1960s. He recalls one customer who bought a gnome which he named Cedric and grew very attached to. One day he came back, with Cedric in tow, to choose another gnome as a friend for Cedric – or rather, for Cedric to choose a friend for himself. It was not a matter, the customer explained, in which he felt he could undertake sole responsibility. Other customers have gone as far as holding a formal wedding ceremony for two gnomes at Gnome World, attending in full rig of morning dress and top hats.

This ability to inspire fantasy is the treasure that today's descendants of the mining spirits of folk tradition dig for. Owners of gnomes often give them names, make up enjoyable stories about them as if they were alive, speculate about what they may get up to when no human eye is on them, take them to bed with them or talk to them when no one else is listening, while realising perfectly well in another part of their minds that gnomes are simply inanimate objects made on a production line in a factory.

ELEMENTAL MY DEAR WATSON

An illustration of religious need underlying fascination with fairyland and its inhabitants is the curious episode of Sir Arthur Conan Doyle and the fairy photographs. The creator of the arch-rational fictional detective Sherlock Holmes, Conan Doyle was a Roman Catholic who became first an atheist and then an ardent believer in Spiritualism. He was sent photographs of fairies, taken in 1917 by two Bradford girls, 16-year-old Elsie Wright and her 10-year-old cousin Frances Griffiths, at Cottingley Dell, near Bingley in Yorkshire. The two girls had been telling their incredulous families for some time that they had seen fairies dancing in the dell.

LEFT
A surprising number of quite eminent and otherwise rational people are said to have believed in fairies

FAIRIES AT THE BOTTOM OF THE GARDEN

The girls had then drawn figures of butterfly-winged fairies, cut them out and fastened them to toadstools with hatpins to make it look as if the fairies were dancing on them, and taken the photographs. Elsie's father, who developed the negatives, was disbelieving, but her mother mentioned them at a Spiritualist meeting and they came to Conan Doyle's attention. He saw them as evidence of spirits taking visible form and so as confirmation of the claims of mediums to summon the spirits of the dead to visible appearance. He had the photographs checked by Kodak, who were sceptical but could find no hard evidence of tampering. In 1921 a clairvoyant went to the dell with the girls several times and said he saw fairies, gnomes, elves, brownies and goblins there.

In 1922 Conan Doyle published a book in which he took the photographs seriously, *The Coming of the Fairies*. The girls were reluctant to embarrass Conan Doyle, and Frances always insisted the fairies were real, but in 1983 Elsie finally came clean and admitted the hoax.

In the same book Conan Doyle also took seriously the experiences reported by a Miss Winter of Blarney in Ireland – a shade unfortunately perhaps – who claimed that her family had been in touch with a leprechaun called Bebel. He was fond of the children, and the adults often listened to them talking cheerfully with the little fellow, who told them how fairies liked to ride on hens' backs and hated being chased by dogs. There were leprechauns of both sexes, apparently, ruled by Queen Picel, who flew around on a dragonfly.

FREEDOM FOR GNOMES

Their ability to instil enjoyable fantasies has made gnomes the victims of students' protests, rag weeks and charity fund-raising stunts, and they have been seen chained to railings to demonstrate, sufragette-like, against their unjust exclusion from the Chelsea Flower Show. Some years ago a group of Oxford undergraduates concocted the engaging fantasy of the gnome graveyard, to which all gnomes go to die when their time comes. The students surreptitiously kidnapped gnomes from local gardens and assembled them all in an abandoned quarry – the gnome graveyard – before anonymously ringing the police. They had conscientiously hung a luggage label on each gnome giving his home address, so that the gnomes could all be returned safely to their grieving owners.

Early in 1997 the Garden Gnome Liberation Front in France hit the headlines after over 30 gnomes mysteriously appeared in woodland near the quiet Normandy town of Alençon. They had been kidnapped from their homes and, according to the Front, given back their liberty, freed from their miserable solitude and restored to their natural habitat in the forest. Some had been repainted and relieved of their red caps, which the Front regarded as humiliating badges of servitude. The Front, believed to be students, operate commando-style raids under cover of sinister disguises. They claim to operate in groups of seven out of respect for Snow White's dwarfs, and have so far avoided arrest – but only because owners are reluctant to file complaints about garden-dwarf napping. The daring raiders have also struck in Rennes and Caen.

LITTLE-GNOME FACT

By remarkable coincidence, Alençon, home of the notorious *Front de Libération des Nains de Jardin*, is twinned with the Hampshire town of Basingstoke, home of the publishers of this tribute to gnomes.

BELOW & RIGHT
The black-hooded Garden Gnome Liberation Front, with some of their newly liberated 'victims'

Above
They're no trouble… really, pleads Mr and Mrs Raymond's daughter, Yvonne Evans

Dedicated Gnome-owners

Happy in the grip of pleasurable fantasy, some gnome-owners build up remarkably large collections. In the 1980s and '90s people would come from all over the world to marvel at a crew of almost 200 gnomes, of all sizes and types, which belonged to Mr and Mrs Granville Raymond of Haverfordwest in Wales. Exactly how many gnomes there were was always in some doubt, as there were 'naughty' ones which ran off into the shrubbery and might not reappear. Mrs Raymond made them summer sun hats and they had sou'westers for rainy days and special outfits in which to celebrate Christmas Day and St David's Day. Admirers from as far away as Australia would send them Christmas cards and woolly hats for the winter, while one part of the garden was a refuge for gnomes brought in by owners who had tired of them. One of the gnomes, named Roy, went off on active service to Bosnia as a Royal Signals Regiment mascot. Unfortunately, the house and garden had to be sold when Mr Raymond died.

Left
Robert Chambers with a couple of his young charges

The British may be renowned around the world for their eccentricity, but they are by no means alone in their foibles and obsessions. You need not travel far before passing colourful collections of gnomes in front gardens, roadsides, and even on traffic roundabouts both in Britain and on mainland Europe. The gnome owners from other countries can be just as passionate about their charges.

ABOVE
Driving along in Krynica, south-east Poland, you may come across these fellows at the Polish Sailors' café; Christmas is a particularly good time, when their owner adds a stable and nativity scene, complete with music

Another distressed gnomes' home and sanctuary was opened in 1996 by Robert Chambers of Duddenhoe End, near Saffron Walden in Essex. Conservative leader of the local district council and winner of the Dunmow Flitch in 1996, he offered refuge in his garden to unwanted gnomes, whose owners wished to be rid of them. Asked by the *Independent* newspaper what attracted him about his charges, Mr Chambers spoke for thousands of gnome fanciers by replying: 'I like them because they are friendly little creatures who always have a smile on their faces…They represent the spirits that live under the soil and look after the plants.'

ABOVE & RIGHT
These happy little fellows have a new home with Robert Chambers

THE INTERNATIONAL GNOME CONVENTION

GNOMES OF THE WORLD UNITED

The year 1995 was important in gnome annals as the year of the first-ever International Gnome Convention, which was held in Christchurch, New Zealand, and which heralded a serious outbreak of gnomical puns. The convention was organised by the New Zealand Gnome Committee, which is strongly 'green' in its sympathies and likes to spell out the word 'gnome' to mean Guarding Naturally Over Mother Earth.

The moving spirit behind the whole occasion was Henry Sunderland, a graphic designer and teacher. German-made garden gnomes seem to have reached Australia and New Zealand in small numbers before the Second World War (not quite as long ago as in the amiable fantasy that the first gnomes arrived with Captain Cook). The gnome population in New Zealand swelled significantly from the early 1950s on, as substantial numbers of English and Dutch settlers arrived, encouraged by the government's immigration policies. They brought their taste in gardens with them and gnomes now began to be seen more often in New Zealand gardens, along with painted rocks, shells and figures of frogs, flamingos and seals balancing silver balls on their noses. Small workshops opened to manufacture gnomes and other garden ornaments. In the 1980s and 90s a flood of cheap mass-produced gnomes started to roll in from Asian manufacturers, while craftspeople in New Zealand turned to designing more refined and imaginative figures to meet a growing demand. In Auckland something called the Dead Gnome Society started selling a special gnome with a knife stuck in his back, as a kitchen knife-holder. You were meant to take the knife out to use it and then simply stab the gnome with it again.

ABOVE
The guest of honour

VERY IMPORTANT GNOMES

Guests of honour at the convention were the Lamport Hall gnome and Terry Major-Ball, John Major's brother and seasoned gnome and garden ornament creator. The venerable Lamport Hall gnome was formally welcomed at Christchurch Airport by a delegation which included gnomes belonging to the mayors of Christchurch and Wellington.

Events at the International Gnome Convention included a gnome fun run and a gnome picnic, lectures, discussions and visits to local places of interest. Gnomes arrived from Britain, Germany, Australia, Japan and Korea, the United States and the United Arab Emirates. Local craftspeople brought figures of their own creation, including up-market ecologically correct gnomes in black hats with flowers, pumpkins, vegetable barrows and baskets of apples, city slicker gnomes on motor bikes, elfin soft toys which you place near ailing plants to cheer them up, and a gnude gnome.

ABOVE
Charlie, huddled against the cold, braves the snows of Antarctica

Christchurch is believed to be the only town in the world with its own official city gnome, and plans are afoot to persuade the American city of Seattle, with which it twinned, to take an official gnome to its municipal heart. It seems fantasy reigns on in the Antipodes.

BELOW LEFT
Henry Sunderland and Charlie, looking a little frosted, record their triumphant arrival at the South Pole

HAVE GNOME WILL TRAVEL

Henry Sunderland, who made history in 1977 by depositing Charlie the gnome at the South Pole, says that the burgeoning interest has gone along with the rise of conservationist concern for Mother Earth, with gnomes seen as guardians of the ecology. A keen conservationist and ardent gnomophile, Henry travelled to Antarctica with Charlie courtesy of the the US Navy and left him in care of kindly scientists at the South Pole as their mascot. Unfortunately, he failed to persuade the RAF and US Air Force to fly Jernome, 'Chair Gnome' of the convention, to the North Pole in the interests of world peace. This was despite Jernome having a special insurance policy covering him against frostbite and being housed in a transparent capsule as a precaution against catching gneumonia.

GNOMIC ATTRACTIONS

BELIEF IN NATURE SPIRITS and the 'little people' has persisted to a surprising extent in what is supposed to be an age of scepticism and materialism. In her 1960s book on Dartmoor folklore, Ruth E St Leger-Gordon remarked that 'the best-known and most popular survival in Dartmoor folklore today is undoubtedly the pixy'. She thought this was largely due to the many outsiders who had come to live in this part of Devon, settling in renovated cottages or modern bungalows which they christened Pixy Dell or Pixy Nook and installing a pixy sitting cross-legged on a toadstool on the lawn. Their influence, she thought, had given new life to a native folk tradition that had been on its last legs.

THE GNOME RESERVE

West Putford, near Bradworthy,
North Devon EX22 7XE.
Telephone: (01409) 241435

SET AMONG QUIET LANES in peaceful north Devon countryside, south of the main A39 road between Bideford and Bude, not far from Clovelly, this is Britain's and the world's major

LEFT
If you go down to the woods today...

ABOVE
Elder gnomes gather for a friendly debate

LEFT
One of the younger residents holds the attention of friends with a good book

gnome tourist attraction. Founded in 1979 by the artist Ann Atkin, three generations of her family are now involved with the site. Its population has grown over the years until there are now more than 1,000 gnomes and pixies assembled here.

Many of them are in an attractive beech wood with a stream running through it as a magnet for fishing gnomes. Others are

Above
Relaxing with a friendly game of cards after a hard day's work down the mines

Top
Gnomes are extremely sociable creatures, often seen in groups

Above
Trophies up for grabs in the tense final of the lawnmower race

stationed in the shade of the trees, cushioned in ivy or moss beside the paths that run through the wood. They are pushing barrows, wielding garden tools or tending birds. Others are riding pigs, playing chess, playing instruments or holding an important ecological conference. Tiny gnomes cheerfully straddle toadstools, and inside a small house four tough miner gnomes are playing cards round a toadstool table, gambling with little chunks of gold. The large wild garden has hundreds of species of wild flowers, herbs, ferns and grasses, and small children can go into a simulated pixie dwelling inside a flower stem.

Gnome For a Day

Visitors are issued with red gnome caps, which they are encouraged to wear.

Although not compulsory, the Reserve likes people to don them – and, however sheepishly, almost everyone does – ostensibly on the grounds that it makes the resident gnomes feel less self-conscious. But actually it is because the caps make the visitors themselves less self-conscious and able to enter more easily into the spirit of the place. Reactions to putting on the caps range from hysterical giggles to preternatural solemnity. Like party hats or masks, the caps break down barriers between people and generations, and take you out of your ordinary conventional self and into a different zone. Visitors often say that they feel a visit to the Gnome Reserve inculcates a better sense of proportion.

The Reserve publishes the occasional *Gnome News*, with its engaging slogan – 'Gnome News Is Good News' – and makes its own pixies for sale; visitors can see them being made. There are about 25,000 visitors a year, mostly British, but with some Americans and some Dutch, who are particularly fond of gnomes. Gnomes, Ann Atkin says, are 100 per cent humorous and 100 per cent serious at the same time. They are symbols of a force deep in human nature and in the world at large, whose influence is towards a sense of wholeness and a realisation of the folly of destroying the environment.

LEFT
Tiny pixies on sale

RIGHT
Gather ye mushrooms while ye may

BELOW
A glass or two of the local cider is always on offer in the West Country, but beware its effects

GNOME WORLD

Moorland Road, Indian Queens,
Cornwall TR9 6HN.
Telephone: (01726) 860812

ALAN QUARTERMAN has been making and selling concrete gnomes here since the early 1960s, and says he calls them gnomes rather than the more usual Cornish piskies because gnomes have beards and piskies do not. In fact, he says, proper Cornish piskies are completely naked except for their hats and boots. He has created a lively gnome garden out of a former field, with getting on for 200 of the little people busy gardening or playing instruments, riding tortoises or fishing in the winding stream.

The setting for Gnome World offers fine views of the spectacular China Clay Country, and features nature trails, a children's playground, a farm shop and a caravan site, and events include traction rallies. Gnome World is sign-posted off the main A30 road between Bodmin and Redruth.

RIGHT
Pick your own mushrooms

BELOW
Relaxing with some fishing among the waterside plants of the gardens

Left
This lucky fellow may well look wide-eyed if his numbers come up on the lottery

Right
The owl and the pussycat… and their kindly companion

Right
A jolly red giant, even down to his boots, welcomes visitors to Gnome World

BELOW
Lord Jack, senior gnome at Pixieland, knowingly twirls his handsome white beard

PIXIELAND

Dartmeet, near Princetown,
Devon PL20 6SG
Telephone: (01364) 631412

ON DARTMOOR, beside the B3357 road west of Dartmeet, and not far from Dartmoor Prison, is Pixieland. Numerous pixies are clustered outside the gift shop, some fishing in a small stream, some sitting on spotted toadstools. Painted concrete pixies have been made here for 50 years or so, with bright red caps and green jackets, white beards, red lips and a spot of red on each cheek. Most are male, including some pixie footballers, but there are a few females.

RIGHT
A tiny pixie enjoys a rest by the roadside on a day out

BELOW
New signings for England, Plymouth Argyll and Manchester United

RIGHT
Pig farming is quite unusual in these parts

WATERMOUTH CASTLE

Near Ilfracombe, North Devon EX34 9SL
Telephone: (01271) 8643879

BELOW
Norman the gnome greets a young visitor

BOTTOM
A strange figure lurks behind the hedge

ON THE COAST road between Ilfracombe and Combe Martin, this imposing castellated mansion dates from the 1820s and belonged to the Bassetts for a century. By the time the Haines family bought it in 1977, the house was dilapidated and the grounds were a jungle, but they have successfully restored the place as a theme park for families with children. It all began with the purchase of a job lot of 35 German gnomes who were found languishing idly in Ireland. The Haines family brought them over to Devon and built a village for them.

Some 150,000 visitors a year, including many from Holland, Germany and Austria, come to enjoy Gnomeland as well as the spectacular water show with light and music effects, the enchanted walk, haunted mill, snake tube slide, maze and carousel. Also on offer are a model railway layout, doll and mechanical music collections, Victorian kitchen and scenes from Edwardian life, smugglers' dungeon, Snow White and the seven dwarfs, Gulliver in Lilliput and other attractions.

Other features at Gnomeland include a mine entrance and a troll's cave; visitors peep through the windows of the houses to see animated scenes of gnome family life inside, involving gnome fathers, mothers, children and babies. Children can pan for gold and be photographed with an actor dressed as Norman Gnome, and there is also a gnome shop selling all sorts of souvenirs and goodies to complete an unusual fantasy day out for the whole family.

ABOVE
High jinks in the sawmill and workshop

BELOW
The animated gnomes are a major attraction

Related Fairylands

De Efteling

Kaatsheuvel, Holland, north of Tilburg, off the N261

This massive leisure and fantasy park or 'walk-through picture book' in the south-west, which draws some three million visitors a year, opened in 1952. Inspired by the drawings of a Dutch artist, Anton Pieck, the complex was developed around its original Fairytale Wood feature, where the seven dwarfs weep around Snow White's transparent coffin. There are gauzy-winged fairies, singing animals and giant mushrooms playing a tune on a harpsichord. There are numerous scenes from fairy tales and domestic scenes of gnome life. The Troll King sits on his throne and the grotesque, mythical 'people of Laaf' can be seen in their weird and wonderful homes.

Above
Efteling is a huge complex and very popular with visitors of all ages

Right
The nursery at Laafland has an almost surreal quality

DISNEYLAND PARIS

Marne-La-Vallee, some 20 miles (30km) east of Paris

ALTHOUGH NOT strictly in keeping with these other visitor attractions, this theme park, opened in 1992, does have some of the required elements. In Fantasyland, the realm of fairy tales, visitors enter the world of Snow White, see the wicked queen's castle, meet the evil witch herself and take a train ride through the nightmare forest to the dwarfs' diamond mine. Snow White and the dwarfs also appear on stage in the Castle Theatre. Other experiences relate to other well-know children's stories and traditional fairy tales.

LEFT & BELOW

The fairy king Oberon and his friends; more Laafs, this time at work in the bakery

Above & Right Despite its small size, the Gnome Museum manages to cram in an awful lot of gnomes

Das Deutsche Gartenzwerg Museum,

D-74583 Rot am See, Germany, on the B6 between Nuremberg and Heilbronn
Telephone: (07955) 3021

The first German Garden Gnome Museum was opened in Rot am See, in the Kreis Schwäbish Hall, on 3 October 1991, the first day of Germany's reunification. It is run by the non-profit-making association of Das Deutsche Gartenzwerg-Museum, founded earlier that year on 3 August by Günter and Jutta Griebel. All income from the museum is ploughed into this association, and thus back into the museum itself. Günter Griebel, also chairman of the association, is a specialist on 'nanology' – the study of dwarfs.

One of the pioneers of the German garden gnome was Phillipp Griebel, who founded his factory in Gräfenroda in Thüringia – traditional home of the original garden dwarf ornaments – in 1874. With gnomes enjoying renewed status as cult items, Das ZwergenKaufhaus, the Gnome Store, was established in 1987, followed by the Museum. The store traded on the old tradition of manufacturing 'classic' garden gnomes, continuing the work of the original company, resurrected by Phillip's great-grandson Günter and his cousin Reinhard. The

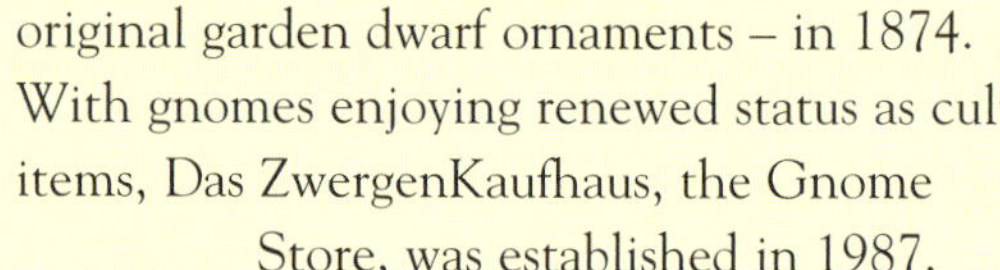

BELOW

A portrayal of the beautiful Snow White, her striking black hair a little reminiscent of Cleopatra, surrounded by her little friends

BELOW

Domestic harmony in a woodland tableau

ABOVE & RIGHT

Gnomes are no respecters of privacy

Griebels' support for and proliferation of gnomes has resulted in maintaining a high-profile for the creatures in the media.

Today Jutta and Günter's store and museum offer expertise for special gnome orders, and various examples of their wide range of wares have appeared in films, on television and in exhibitions. The collection has grown into the most comprehensive on the subject of gnomes and related little people, and includes extensive archive material and a total of almost 8,000 items.

A number of other, perhaps more mainstream, museums have exhibited items from this collection, and the Gnome Museum itself stages numerous gnome-related projects, often running concurrently. Chief among these is the annual festival, held on the anniversary of German reunification and the foundation of the museum, which represents a unique showcase for leading nanologists from all over the world.

Above
Detail from one of the more unusual exhibits in the museum, a rather charming woodland creature

Above
The museum's Modern Gnome Room has a somwhat minimalist look about it – not unlike other, more mainstream galleries

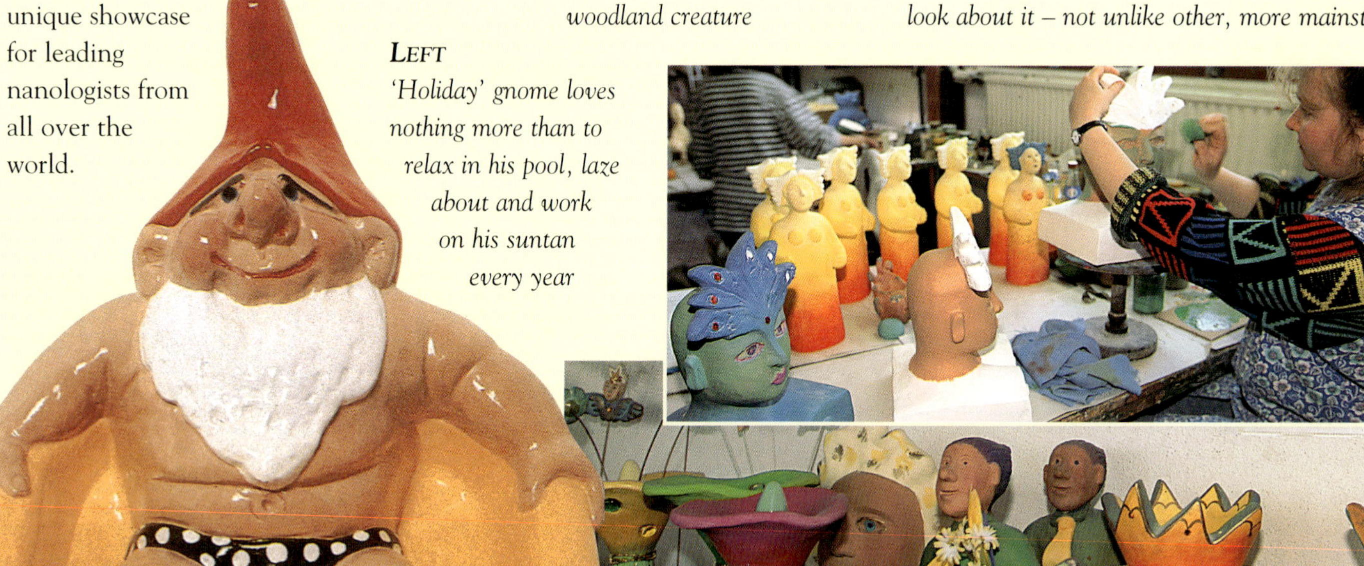

Left
'Holiday' gnome loves nothing more than to relax in his pool, laze about and work on his suntan every year

Left & Below
The new, innovative design of gnome is proving a great success

Gnomes and Culture

The provenance of dwarfs and other little people may lie in European folk tales, but they have survived the centuries through frequent appearances in literature, art and music, and have moved into the modern media of films and television.

A MIDSUMMER NIGHT'S DREAM

FAIRY TRADITIONS have shown themselves remarkably resilient. The fairies in Shakespeare's delightful *A Midsummer Night's Dream*, which features Oberon and Titania, King and Queen of the fairies, are diminutive in stature. Proud Queen Titania's elves take refuge in acorn cups and have names like Cobweb, Peaseblossom, Moth and Mustardseed – all of which had roles in traditional medicine. On the other hand, Titania is large enough to take a human lover in her arms.

Shakespeare's fairies are not sugary nor just miniature humans; there is an eeriness about them and they have formidable powers. There was a strong fertility theme that has linked the fair Titania to the May Queen and the Summer Lady, and Oberon to the May King, in the traditional rites and celebrations that had for centuries ushered in the summer in the English countryside As in popular tradition Shakespeare's fairies dance in circles.

Oberon's court jester, the mischievous Puck – also called Hobgoblin or known by the cautiously propitiatory name of Robin Goodfellow – is the traditional brownie or pixy, a shrewd, knavish sprite who plays pranks on dairymaids and housewives, leads travellers astray, while bringing good luck to those who treat him well. A 17th-century poem mentions Robin Goodfellow's characteristic 'ho ho ho' laugh (appropriated later by Santa Claus), and the modern garden gnome's propensity for cheeriness may owe something to him.

ABOVE
The Royal Ballet's Sarah Wilder and William Trevitt perform 'The Dream'

LEFT
The Quarrel of Oberon and Titania

Fairies and elves also appear in Shakespeare's *The Merry Wives of Windsor* and *The Tempest*, which mentions elves who make fairy rings by moonlight and 'midnight mushrooms' that appear overnight. A mushroom, neatly set with a cloth of white rose-petals, serves as the table for a fairy banquet in 'Britannia's Pastorals' by a Devonshire poet, William Browne, and the mushroom turns up again as the table for a fairy banquet in Robert Herrick's poem 'Oberon's Feast'. Gnomes had a close connection with fertility, making things grow in the ground, and sheltering beneath mushrooms as evening fell; the mushroom and toadstool have enjoyed a long career as fairy and gnome accompaniments.

Fairies appear again in Michael Drayton's burlesque 1627 poem 'Nimphidia', where the fairy queen, Mab, and her ladies are so tiny that they can all find shelter in the bell of a cowslip. Evident here and in Shakespeare are long-lived characteristics of fairy lore, which survive among today's garden gnomes: the charm of smallness, the amused protective affection it arouses, and the association of the little people with flowers and small animals.

There was a significant development right at the end of the 17th century in France, when fairies drawn from folk traditions became fashionable at the court of the Sun King, Louis XIV. Charles Perrault published a collection of stories subtitled *Contes de Ma Mère l'Oye*, 'Tales of Mother Goose'. These included stories which would become famous all over the western world: *Cinderella*, *Red Riding Hood*, *Sleeping Beauty*, *Puss in Boots*, *Bluebeard* and *Hop o' My Thumb*. They were based on genuine folk tales and told in a simple, straightforward style, but Perrault removed crudities and cruelties, ironed out inconsistencies, added fairy godmothers and other characters of his own, and gave them a sophisticated, urbane humour, adding a little moral at the end of each story.

LEFT
Gnomes have a great affinity with mushrooms and toad-stools

THE ORIGIN OF SPECIES

Meanwhile, the elemental gnomes of Paracelsus had made their bow in English literature in 1714, in the second version of Alexander Pope's 'heroi-comical' poem *The Rape of the Lock*. Here the four Elements are inhabited by Spirits, called Sylphs, Gnomes, Nymphs and Salamanders. The Gnomes or Daemons of the Earth delight in mischief; but the Sylphs, who inhabit the air, are the best-disposed creatures imaginable.

In the poem the 'dusky and melancholy' gnome Umbriel describes the mischievous brownie-like tricks he has played in the past: planting pimples on pretty faces, rumpling pettticoats and tumbling beds, fixing horns to heads and inflicting diseases on costly lapdogs.

Pope certainly did not believe in his gnomes and sylphs, which appear for amusement and satirical purposes only, but the charming little airy sylphs, fluttering protectively about the heroine and called variously fays, fairies and elves, may well have been responsible for the later tendency to equip fairies with wings.

Gnomes, sylphs and the other elemental spirits reappeared in the 1790s in Erasmus Darwin's long, engaging and, in its time popular, poem *The Botanic Garden*. Darwin was a leading scientist of his day; as well as a much admired physician and inventor he was also the grandfather of the great Charles Darwin. Darwin's gnomes in their 'dusky squadrons' are on hand at the original creation of the earth.

ABOVE
Umbriel, the 'dusky and melancholy' gnome from The Rape of the Lock

LITTLE-GNOME FACT

Umbriel, from Alexander Pope's *The Rape of the Lock*, is literature's first named gnome, the first society gnome and the first gnome with wings. Like the dwarfs of Germanic lore, his proper home is deep in the earth.

HAUNTING TALES

Publishing fiction specifically intended for children had become profitable for the first time and the scene was now set for the creation of the 19th-century fairyland. With the new demand for and supply of published children's reading in the early 19th century, there was a strong accompanying emphasis on instruction and edification. The importance of children's reading in inculcating approved ideas and attitudes was taken just as seriously as it still is today. Fairy godmothers turned into ethics instructors for the nursery and any element of entertainment that survived in the stories tended to be there to sugar the pill of righteousness. The humorous artist and caricaturist George Cruikshank, for example, contrived to turn *Cinderella, Hop o' My Thumb* and *Jack and the Beanstalk* into temperance tracts in his 1850s 'Fairy Library' for children, and was as pained and astonished to be forcefully denounced by Charles Dickens as any politically correct do-gooder of today.

The less didactic, more fanciful, macabre and disturbing aspects of traditional fairy lore had begun to make a comeback with the first of Grimms' tales in English (with illustrations by Cruikshank), followed in 1846 by the first English translation of stories by Hans Christian Andersen. Born in 1805 in a slum at Odense in Denmark, where his birthplace is now a shrine to him, Andersen heard some of his tales as a child from an old local woman; others he invented. He published his first fairy tales for children in 1835 and his famous *The Little Mermaid* appeared in 1837.

Andersen dropped the 'for children' label and his admirers treat the stories as being as much for adults as for the young. They outshone his novels in popularity and esteem, and made him famous far beyond Denmark. Never an easy or happy man, when he died in 1875 he was Denmark's most successful and revered author, and he still is. Andersen's tales were infused with a moral purpose which appealed to conventional Victorian parents, while being spiced with lively fantasy and an attractive humorous touch.

ABOVE
Hans Christian Andersen (1805–75), the son of a shoemaker, was once refused work in the theatre for his lack of education

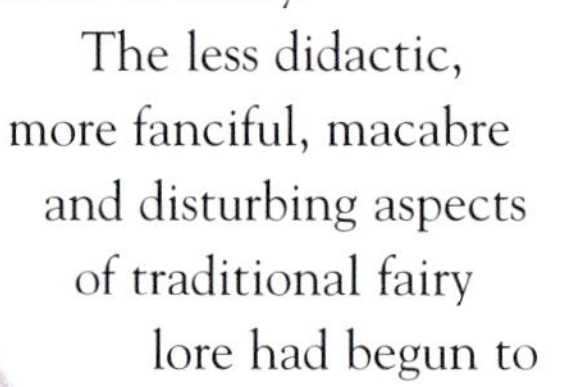

RIGHT
Edvard Erichsen's bronze statue of Andersen's character 'The Little Mermaid', unveiled in 1913, is one of Copenhagen's main tourist attractions

ABOVE
The unmistakable style of Arthur Rackham brings to life Ibsen's Peer Gynt

LEFT
A minstrel-type gnome of the past may have regaled audiences with folk tales and songs

Strange and haunting, and again not directed at children, are the plays *Brand* and *Peer Gynt*, written in 1866 and 1867 by Henrik Ibsen. Through these he brought the troll traditions of his native Norway into international literature. Ibsen was powerfully influenced by the Scandinavian sagas and the folk tales collected by Asbjörnsen and Moe. In 1862 he went collecting folk ballads and stories in the Norwegian countryside himself before leaving Norway for years of exile in Italy and Germany. The action of Peer Gynt and his dealings with the Old Man of the Mountains – the troll-king – and his daughter covers some 50 years from early in the 19th century. Ibsen told his publisher that Peer Gynt was originally a real man, who had lived in the Gulbrand Valley district around 1800 and tales were still told of him there. The play owes several of its themes to Asbjörnsen and Moe, with the trolls representing the forces of evil.

LITERARY GIANTS

British 19th-century authors who mined the gold of the fairy tale genre included Coleridge, Shelley, Keats, Lamb, Thackeray, Ruskin, Charles Kingsley, Tennyson, Lewis Carroll and Oscar Wilde, and many others whose names and work are forgotten today. Edward Knatchbull-Hugessen, for instance, a Liberal politician who was created Lord Brabourne in 1880, had published children's fairy tales in the previous two decades. An 1871 story, *Charlie and the Elves*, is about a small boy who finds himself trapped in a big cobweb by a crew of triumphant little people. They take him away to their own realm and show their prize to the chief elf, clothed from head to foot in green.

By the turn of the century, while the gnome had made his bow as a fairytale presence in the garden, English publishers were making healthy profits out of illustrated versions of the classic fairy tales. An excessive reverence for childhood as a state of primal innocence turned the earthy, formidable little people of folk tradition into mimsy, saccharine sprites, flitting about from petal to petal on butterfly or dragonfly wings. The most influential figure in this sentimentalising and trivialising process was J M Barrie. *Peter Pan*, his disturbing masterpiece, was first staged in London in 1904. It was an instant, huge success, with its boy-hero who could not grow up, its spectacular flying sequences, its lost children and its urgent demand at the play's central crisis that the children in the audience save the languishing Tinkerbell by proclaiming their belief in fairies.

The play soon conquered America as well, and has been standard children's fare ever since. Barrie followed up with *Peter Pan in Kensington Gardens* in 1906 and in 1911 published the play in book form as Peter and Wendy. He also paid for the 'Peter Pan' statue in Kensington Gardens by Sir George Frampton, with its winged fairies, rabbits, mice, birds

BELOW
Sir George Frampton's charming statue, commemorating J M Barrie's eternal boy hero, is a popular feature in Kensington Gardens, London

ABOVE
'They saw a small, brown, pointy-eared person...', from Puck of Pook's Hill

RIGHT
Tolkien found influence in mythological tales like that of the dwarf-lord Alberich

LEFT
If you listen very hard, you may hear the sound of dwarfs and elves moving around under foot

and a squirrel. Erected in 1912, it is one of London's most popular statues. It was in this atmosphere that garden gnomes gained their initial popularity on the English scene, and there is little doubt that whimsicality and the roguish puckishness of these little red-capped figures were major factors in their appeal.

Edwardian sprites were given a fearsome walloping by Rudyard Kipling, who resurrected the traditional Puck in *Puck of Pook's Hill*, published in 1906, the year before he won the Nobel Prize for Literature. Puck appears to two children who have been acting out part of *A Midsummer Night's Dream*, 'a small, brown, broad-shouldered, pointy-eared person with a snub nose, slanting blue eyes, and a grin that ran right across his freckled face.' He wears a dark blue cap like a columbine flower, and his feet are bare and hairy.

ELFIN MAGIC

The year 1937 heralded the publication of *The Hobbit* by J R R Tolkien. Born in South Africa in 1892, of mixed German and English ancestry, Tolkien, who started inventing languages in his teens, became a distinguished academic authority on Anglo-Saxon, Middle English and Old Norse, holding professorial chairs at Oxford University. He created a rich mythological world, set in what he called 'the Elder Days' or 'the First Age of the World', founded on Germanic and Norse mythology and tradition, with its own languages and magic runes, its own heroic monarchs of yore, its high and stately elves, its evil monsters, its legends and lore. One evening in the 1920s he was sitting at home drearily marking examination papers when he wrote down on a blank piece of paper the sentence: 'In a hole in the ground there lived a hobbit.' What this meant, or what a hobbit was, he did not know, but in time he began telling his children a story about a hobbit and the sentence survived to be the opening one of the book.

Tolkien's hobbits are an engaging cross between human beings and the brownie or puckish type of traditional fairy. They are a diminutive race, good-natured and much given to laughter, they smoke pipes and blow smoke-rings, enjoy their food and tend to have comfortable stomachs. They dress in bright green and yellow, but wear no shoes because their feet have leathery soles and are covered with thick brown hair. The dwarfs all play musical instruments and sing beautifully of their ancestral home in deep caverns beneath the far Misty Mountains, where under their ruler, the King under the Mountain, they made great works of skilled craftsmanship, wonderful

swords, golden crowns and silver necklaces for many an ancient monarch and elvish lord, and golden goblets and harps for themselves. The whole adventure is inspired by the powerful wizard Gandalf, whose name also comes from the Icelandic sources (it means 'magician-elf').

Tolkien went on to create his magnificent three-volume epic *The Lord of the Rings*, (1954–55), a titanic contest between the forces of good and evil. Tolkien did not imagine that hobbits or elves or dwarfs were real, or ever had been, but he did think that there was profound truth in his mythical world.

The Tolkien books achieved a cult status in the 1960s, especially on American university campuses – 'Tolkien Is Hobbit-Forming', the lapel badges said. The books were translated into numerous languages and they inspired a fresh and vigorous wave of fantasy and 'sword and sorcery' fiction. An animated film version of *The Lord of the Rings* was released in part in the 1970s and in 1997 it was ranked the greatest book of the 20th century in a British poll in which more than 25,000 people voted.

The Noddy Phenomenon

A diminutive hero of a very different stamp is Enid Blyton's elfin Noddy and his friend Big Ears – a garden gnome with outsize aural appendages. Born in 1897 in London, Blyton dropped her youthful ambition to be a concert pianist and began writing stories and poems. Drawings of figures by a Dutch artist named Harmsen Van Der Beek, which were being used as illustrations in booklets given away free with jars of jam, set her off imagining stories and characters: the result was the adventures of Little Noddy, Big Ears the Pixy and the teddy bears Mr and Mrs Tubby. They, the policeman Mr Plod and the other inhabitants of Toyland became favourites in picture books for younger children and familiar characters in a cartoon strip in the London *Evening Standard* as well as in children's programmes on television, on the backs of cereal packets and in the *Noddy in Toyland* Christmas pantomime, which began in the 1950s and was later filmed.

Van Der Beek began to be haunted at his work by disquieting visions of Little Noddies crawling all over his desk. He died in 1953, but the Noddy bandwagon rolled on, spawning a formidable array of merchandising products which capitalised on the diminutive, elvish hero, with his round face and little button nose, his blue cap with a gold bobble on the end and his customary expression of bemused astonishment. Translated into languages ranging from Icelandic to Arabic, he carried all before him as 'Oui Oui' in France. Early on he was mostly a silly Noddy, a taxi-driver, careering about in his little car, getting into endless scrapes, to the irritation of every-one, including sometimes even the amiable, ever-smiling Big Ears, with his white beard and whiskers, who lived in a toadstool house and rode a bicycle. The stories also featured a Dark Wood populated by nasty goblins, Sly and Gobbo among them. The fact that Toyland swarmed with golliwogs, some of them of villainous inclination, did nothing to endear the stories to the politically correct, and they have been quietly purged from the more recent revisions of the texts.

Left
An engaging pantomime performance featuring Noddy and his companion Big Ears

Below
This fellow definitely has a stage presence about him

A MUSICAL HERITAGE

Munich in 1869 saw the first performance of Das Rheingold, the first of Richard Wagner's Ring operas (see page 11). In 1848 he had written an outline for an opera based on the myth of the Nibelungs, metalworkers living in subterranean caverns, feverishly burrowing in the earth. The entire project took 26 years to complete, and the premiere of the cycle was staged at Bayreuth in 1876. The complex plot of the *Ring* cycle is based on the *Nibelungenlied* and the Scandinavian sagas.

The basic tale of a magic ring of power owned deep underground by a shape-changing dwarf, who puts a fatal curse on it, comes from Snorri Sturluson, but as always Wagner used his source material to create something new and immeasurably powerful of his own. The black elf Alberich of the saga is a vicious tyrant, unable to feel love or compassion for anyone. His brother Mime, who is so often played on the stage as a pathetic character the audience should pity, was intended to be despicably evil and cowardly. Indeed, Wagner describes him as small and bent, hobbling and deformed, with a harsh voice, an abnormally large head, piercing little eyes, a long grey beard and a bald head, covered by a red cap.

James Scott Skinner, a Scottish fiddle-player and prolific composer known as the 'Strathspey King', composed a melody called *Haunt of the Gnomes*. Despite their propensity for playing musical instruments, recognised gnome bands or orchestras are lacking.

However, there is something distinctly gnomish about the Smurfs, who, like gnomes, are loved by some, but stir up feelings of loathing in others. They were invented in Belgium in the 1950s by a cartoonist named Peyo. Little blue, grinning creatures with squeaky voices and pointed caps, they make records in which they replace the lyrics of well-known pop songs with the word 'Smurf'. They had three records in the Top Twenty in Britain in 1978 and sales of little Smurf figures in Europe at large were running at 250,000 a week for a while. After disappearing from the music scene soon after that, they came squeaking back in the mid-1990s with an album titled 'Smurfs Go Pop' (as one journalist said, 'If only they would!'). As with other notable bands, The Smurfs enjoyed fame in their own television series, pitting their wits against the evil Gargamel.

LITTLE-GNOME FACT

Probably the most famous musical gnomic tribute, David Bowie's *Laughing Gnome*, chuckled his way to number six in the British singles chart in 1973, in a stay of 12 weeks.

RIGHT
Gnomes are much given to music-making, but with singularly little recognition

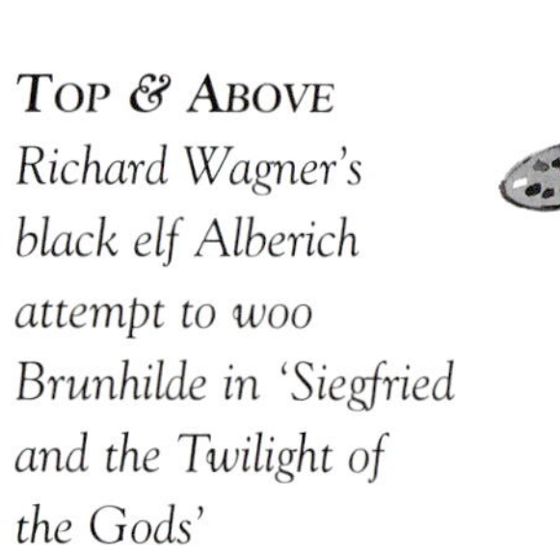

TOP & ABOVE
Richard Wagner's black elf Alberich attempt to woo Brunhilde in 'Siegfried and the Twilight of the Gods'

LEFT & BELOW
A colourful, fun production by David Wood (left), and Alan Ayckbourn's Time and Time Again *(below)*

STAGE GNOMES

The 'little people' or diminutive fairies who are the ancestors of today's garden gnomes appeared on the English stage for the first time in the Elizabethan period, in 1591 in John Lyly's *Endimion*, when they came on briefly to punish one of the characters by pinching him black and blue (and are thought to have been played by the smallest children at the St Paul's Cathedral choir school).

A musical family Christmas show by David Wood called *The Ideal Gnome Exhibition* did the rounds in the 1990s. The plot involves two gnomes called Mr Fisher and Mr Wheeler. They set out on an adventure while their owners, the Big Ones, are away on holiday, and meet a talking pneumatic drill and other characters. Not to be outdone, celebrated playwright Alan Ayckbourn's comedy *Time and Time Again* features a character given to holding conversations with a somewhat surprising garden gnome.

GNOME NEWS IS GOOD NEWS

Gnomes are hardly out of the newspapers these days, or so it seems, with even prestigious authorities like Reuters unable to resist the latest antics of the Gnome Liberation Front. Not content to be hidden away in gardening magazines, gnome mania is rife in the quality press. Newspapers like *The Independent*, *The Guardian*, *Observer* and even the *Sunday Telegraph Magazine* have all covered stories of the little creatures, with tales of kidnapping, abandonment, sanctuaries, snobbery and disapproval. Not to be outdone, local papers like the *Basingstoke Gazette* and the *Woking Review*, from the heart of the Home Counties, have also been gripped by news of gnomic appearances and adventures.

At a more elevated level, Lord Gnome is the imaginary tycoon-proprietor of *Private Eye*, and the old link between gnomes and mining for gold resurfaced in the phrase 'gnomes of Zurich', applied to influential Swiss bankers who were alleged to be causing the British government serious financial problems in the 1960s. *The New Statesman* in 1964 referred to 'the gnomes of Zurich and their related goblins in the more politically involved capitals.'

LEFT
A starring role for gnomekind with Victor Meldrew and his long-suffering wife in One Foot in the Grave

BELOW
This weird creature and his companions wreaked havoc in Gremlins *and its sequel*

MAKING MISCHIEF

The related goblins could perhaps include gremlins, who are an example of the ancient, deeply rooted human tendency to find an explanation for inexplicable mishaps by attributing them to the activities of spirits. It was unseen, mischievous, gnome-like gremlins who caused things to go wrong with aircraft during the Second World War. They were apparently first invented, or recognised, by First World War naval aviators and their name was said to mean the goblins who came out of Fremlin beer bottles. According to an article in *The Spectator* in 1943, gremlins are small beings, about a foot high, clad in red jackets and green breeches. They have no wings and can fly only as passengers.

One notable sighting of a gremlin was made by William Shatner (later to find fame as Captain Kirk in *Star Trek*) early in his career, as an airline passenger terrified out of his wits by a vicious creature causing destruction to the aeroplane in an episode of the classic series *The Twilight Zone*.

Nowadays gremlins are blamed for mysterious mechanical failings in computers, while scientists have given the name 'red elves' to strange forms of lightning high in the atmosphere above thunderstorms, described by pilots as huge nebulous red flashes or glows shaped like carrots or sometimes like jellyfish, trailing blue tentacles.

NEVER ACT WITH CHILDREN, DOGS...OR GNOMES

Archetypal or not, gnomes bob up in today's world of popular entertainment fairly regularly. They have made their way into episodes of many popular British television programmes, including *Coronation Street*, *Fawlty Towers* and *One Foot in the Grave*. Until his premature departure from 'The Street' in 1997, Derek Wilton, the gnome-obsessed character played by Peter Baldwin, captured the nation's attention with the antics of one of his beloved gnomes – Arthur, companion to Quenevere. Cruelly kidnapped from the garden shared by Derek and his wife Mavis (Thelma Barlow), mysterious postcards, ransom notes and Godfather-like packages were received periodically, and numerous neighbours suspected. In the 1960s British television experienced half a dozen episodes of a programme called *The Gnomes of Dulwich*, in which Terry Scott and

Hugh Lloyd played South London concrete garden gnomes, who commented on the peculiarities of human beings (who did not appear) while keeping up a snobbish rivalry with the plastic gnomes in the garden next door.

Animated Antics

Meanwhile, across the Atlantic, J M Barrie's formula of fantasy, sentimentality and whimsy blended with terror was brewed up again to potent effect by Walt Disney, whose version of the 'Snow White' story was to be one of the great children's classics of the 20th century. *Snow White and the Seven Dwarfs* was released just in time for the Christmas of 1937 in Los Angeles. It was the first American full-length feature film in cartoon form and it also broke new ground by including human characters as well as animals. The huge project involved some 750 animators to create the two million drawings required for the running length of 83 minutes, and no fewer than eight writers were credited with the screenplay, based on the Brothers Grimm. Opinion in Hollywood was convinced that 'Disney's Folly' would be a flop but, although costing $1.5 million to make, the film was a critical and box-office success which took more than $8 million dollars on first release and has been profitable ever since.

The seven dwarfs were named for the film, as Doc, Sleepy, Sneezy, Grumpy, Happy, Bashful and Dopey, so as to give them quickly identifiable individual characters. Bashful is always blushing, Sleepy snoozing off, and so on. Doc, the bespectacled leader, is dignified to the point of pomposity. Disney had hoped to get Arthur Rackham involved and, although this came to nothing, some of the film's frightening scenes, which were so chilling that Disney received hundreds of protesting letters and in England the film was at first banned for under-16s, have a Rackhamish flavour. Hollywood awarded Disney a special Oscar for his work in 1939, or rather a full-sized Oscar accompanied by seven smaller ones for the

Right
This gnome is doing a great impersonation of the Chelsea manager Ruud Gullit

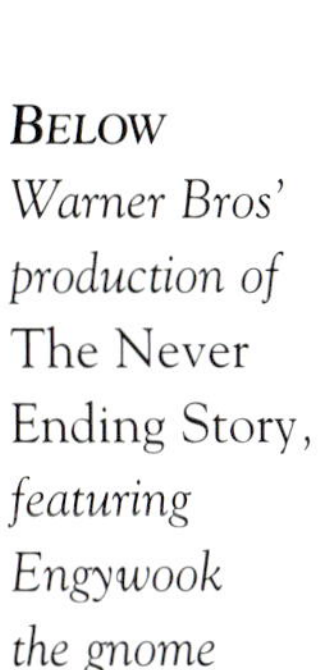

Below
Warner Bros' production of The Never Ending Story, *featuring Engywook the gnome*

Below
The children's television programme, Chish 'n Fips, *featured two helpful garden gnomes*

Above
Another fine mess for Oliver Hardy's gnomesake, one of a famous pair

dwarfs, presented by Shirley Temple. The film's popularity in Europe over the last 60 years or so has almost certainly boosted the appetite for garden gnomes, some of whom today have a Disneyesque look.

The dwarfs' diamond mine was included in the Snow White adventure ride when the original Disneyland opened in California, and the dwarfs can be seen cavorting merrily with the other familiar characters at Disneyworld in Florida today. 'Blanche-Neige et les Sept Nains' is one of the attractions at Disneyworld Paris and the dwarfs are gathered mourning round Snow White's body in her transparent glass coffin in the 'Fairytale Wood' at the Efteling theme park in Holland.

Movie Magic

Paramount tried to cash in with its own *Gulliver's Travels* in 1939, but the Lilliputians proved no match for Doc and the gang, and in *The Wizard of Oz* in the same year, where Judy Garland as Dorothy, the heroine, found herself in Munchkin Land, the diminutive Munchkins, played by a troupe of midgets, made no great impression. Disney bought the rights to *Peter Pan* in 1939, but the film did not come out until 1953, after various Broadway musical treatments had appeared, including one with incidental music by Leonard Bernstein. A notable musical version with Mary Martin as Peter Pan opened in 1954 and there was a 1976 television adaptation which starred Mia Farrow and Danny Kaye.

Above
A young Petula Clark starred with leprechaun Tommy Steele in Finian's Rainbow

In the same general field, *Finian's Rainbow*, a hit Broadway musical about a leprechaun from Ireland, who goes to America to recover a stolen crock of gold, opened in 1947. Bing Crosby recorded *How Are Things in Glocca Morra?* and the film version with Fred Astaire and Petula Clark was released in 1968: Tommy Steele played the leprechaun.

The idiotic film of *Snow White and the Three Stooges* appeared in 1961, with the Olympic skating champion Carol Heiss as the heroine, succoured by the Stooges – the seven dwarfs are away toiling in King Solomon's Mines – while a German film of *Schneewittchen und die Sieben Zwerge*, based on the Grimm original and with Elke Arendt as Snowdrop, was released in 1956.

PAST, PRESENT AND FUTURE

While much of the works featuring gnomes and the little people has tended to be rather serious, author Terry Pratchett, on the other hand, has turned all the traditions of fairyland to humorous account in fantasies set in his 'Discworld', home to a riotous crew of gods, wizards, witches, Death, druids, demons, valkyries, dragons, vampires, spectres, fairy folk and assorted supernatural beings. The first Discworld book, *The Colour of Magic*, was published in 1983.

The smallest species in Discworld are the thievish gnomes and goblins: here a gnome is defined as an underground goblin, and a goblin as a gnome who has come up for air. The dwarfs are stocky and bearded, stand about 4 feet (1.2m) tall and live to be 300 years or so old. They inhabit mountains and mines, are ruled by a king and wear up to twelve layers of clothing, and their dwarf bread, though boring to eat, sustains them for days. They include an adopted dwarf called Carrot Ironfoundperson and Count Giacomo Casanunda, the great lover and liar. The trolls are animated stone creatures who get larger and slower with age, and there are beings called gnolls, which are trolls without the latter's intelligence and nobility of character. Pratchett's elves, with their ruling king and queen, are beautiful, cruel and soulless. There is even a character named Noddy in Discoworld: he is part of the Insanity rock-band.

Quite separately, Terry Pratchett also created the Nomes, tiny human-like beings, four inches (10cm) high with large pointed ears, who have been living in our world since their spaceship crashed here 15,000 years ago and have never managed to escape. A television version of their adventures began running in 1992.

And so, in one form and another, in children's stories, in saga, fantasy and humour, in film, on television and the printed page, the little people and fairy folk of age-old European legend and tradition continue triumphantly to survive. As they do equally, of course, in the garden, where the cheerful, indefatigable little red-capped spirit of the earth with his barrow or his fishing rod guards the home and family values, radiates good humour and neighbourliness, and enables his owners to express their own sense of their true selves and their ideals.

LITTLE-GNOME FACT

Names suggested for Walt Disney's *Snow White and the Seven Dwarfs* – but rejected – included Weepy, Thrifty, Gaspy, Awful and Dirty.

LEFT
The leaders of Terry Pratchett's Nomes in Truckers *are Maskin and, unusually, a girl, Grimma*

BELOW
Stan Laurel hasn't a care in the world as he prepares for his holidays away from Ollie

If the Cap Fits

With an increasing number of gnomes featuring in the media, it is no wonder that they are reaching into the subconcious of a great many people, and what better way than through the lucrative field of advertising.

Perhaps because of their homely and unthreatening image, gnomes have appeared in numerous advertising campaigns, as posters or flyers, in newspapers and, more recently, on television. It seems their is no limit to their sales acumen, being used to persuade potential customers to buy all manner of products. The use of gnomes to sell household items and services like washing powder, shoe polish or home insurance is understandable, given their propensity for domestic chores. But gnomes promoting cigarettes or vodka may seem strange, or perhaps just a sign of the times There seems to be no getting away from them, so we may as well accept them.

Below & Right
Norman, the giant AA home insurance gnome, and an early German advertisement for household products

Below
Gnomes helping to promote a more active life

The Gnome Directory

THE GNOME DIRECTORY

The following is no more than a partial list of garden centres, nurseries and shops around the country which sell garden gnomes. As attitudes in the population at large are reflected in the retail trade, some garden centres view gnomes with lofty disdain, while others are more than happy to enter into the spirit of the little people. Gnomes tend to be seasonal items, on sale in the spring and summer, but not always available in winter. Details here were correct at the time of compilation, but outlets open and close and change policy all the time, so it is sensible to telephone for details before you go.

Abercorn Nurseries
Beehive Lane, Chelmsford, Essex.
Tel: (01245) 257938
Gnomes and fencing, sheds, garden sundries.

ACW Garden Centre
Canal Road, Bradford, West Yorkshire.
Tel: (01274) 392344
Also aquatics, sheds, lawnmowers.

Blagdon Water Garden Centre
Bath Road, Upper Langford, Avon BS18 7DN.
Tel: (01934) 852973
Gnomes, fountain and lawn statuary, birds, water-garden equipment.

Cadbury Garden Centre
Congresbury, Bristol BS19 5AA.
Tel: (01934) 876464
Ornaments and garden furniture, also water gardens, fish, aquariums, pets.

Caerphilly Garden Centre
Penrhos, Nantgarw, near Caerphilly, South Wales. Tel: (01222) 861511
Also pets and aquatics.

Colne Valley Garden Centre
Scar Lane, Milnsbridge, Huddersfield, West Yorkshire. Tel: (01484) 656164
Gnomes, ornaments, garden furniture.

Dobbies Garden Craft
Street House Farm, Ponteland, Northumberland. Tel: (01661) 820202
Also aquatics, pet centre.

Dobbies Gardening World
Melville Nursery, Lasswade, Midlothian, Scotland. Tel: 0131 663 1941
And aquatics, birds of prey; Edinburgh Butterfly World.

Garden Care Nurseries Ltd
Langford Bridge, Ongar, Essex.
Tel: (01277) 365485
Concrete products including gnomes, also paving, sheds etc.

The Gnome Reserve
West Putford, near Bradworthy, North Devon EX22 7XE.
Tel: (01409) 241435
Pixies are made and sold here, at the country's leading gnome tourist attraction.
(see pages 96–99)

Gnomesville
North Devon Garden Centre, Strand Lane, Barnstaple, North Devon. Tel: (01271) 23694
Gnomes, garden ornaments and statuary. The garden centre is off the A39 between Barnstaple and Braunton.

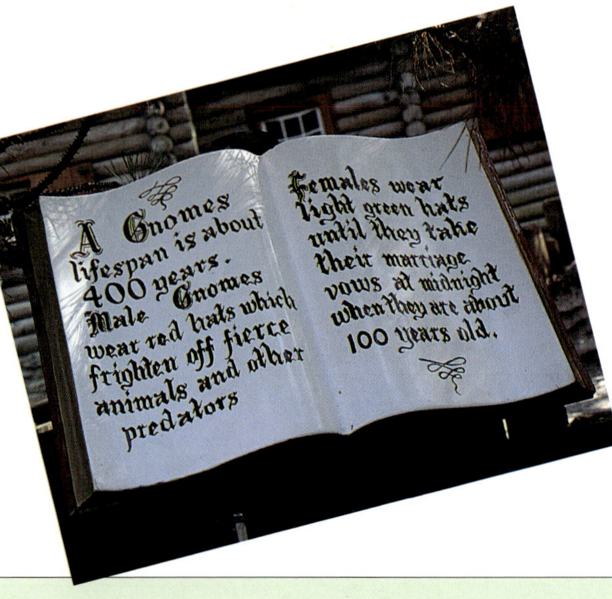

Gnome World
Moorland Road, Indian Queens, Cornwall TR9 6HN.
Tel: (01726) 860812
Concrete gnomes, toadstools, animal figures and bird baths; customised figures can be made to order, within reason; display garden populated by numerous gnomes. Signposted off the A30. (see pages 100–1)

Heighley Gate Nursery Garden Centre
Wooler Road, Morpeth, Northumberland NE61 3DA. Tel: (01670) 513416
Also aquatics, pet centre.

Horseshoe Nurseries
White Elm Road, Bicknacre, Danbury, Essex.
Tel: (01245) 223789
Gnomes and garden ornaments, fish ponds, rockery items.

Limmex Industries
High Street and Wood Street, Swindon, Wiltshire. Tel: (01793) 522056
This delightful, old-fashioned hardware shop in the old centre of Swindon sells the full range of Zeho and Liebermann plastic gnomes, all year round.

Long Street Nursery
Great Ellingham, Norfolk. Tel: (01953) 453175
Gnomes, statues and ornaments, aquatics.; butterfly garden.

The Pixie House and Gift Shop
Penpethy, near Camelford, Cornwall
South of Tintagel on the B3263 road to Camelford. There is a profusion of figures for sale at this roadside 'home of the pixies, gnomes and elves'; also toadstools and animal figures. A Disneyesque, tumbledown pixy house has a gnome peeping out from the chimney.

Pixieland (Garden Ornaments)
Dartmeet, near Princetown, South Devon PL20 6SG. Tel: (01364) 631412
They have been making their own concrete pixies here since the 1940s, and besides their 75 ordinary varieties you can order footballer pixies in the colours of any team you fancy. Also toadstools, animal figures, bird baths, bridges and wishing wells, plus sheep - and goatskin rugs, copper bracelets, bone china, pewter and gifts. On the B3357 west of Dartmeet. (see page 102)

Pugh's Garden Centre
Tynant Nursery, Morganstown, Radyr, Cardiff, South Wales. Tel: (01222) 842017.

Streamline Sales (Mould Manufacturers)
Sedlescombe Road North, St Leonard's-on-Sea, East Sussex TN37 7EJ. Tel: (01424) 442485
Glass fibre, plastic and rubber moulds; sculptor and glass fibre materials. Suppliers of latex mould for pages 70–85.

Tong Garden Centre
Tong Lane, Tong Village, Bradford, West Yorkshire. Tel: (0113) 2853506
Aquatics, patio furniture, fireworks, lawnmowers. Off Wakefield Road.

Torrens Garden Centre
Ashford Road, Bethersden, Kent TN26 3LF. Tel: (01233) 820526
Gnomes, garden ornaments, pets. On the A28 between Bethersden and Tenterden.

Watermouth Castle
Between Ilfracombe and Combe Martin, on the A399 coast road, North Devon EX34 9SL. Tel: (01271) 8643879
Charming, all-weather family fantasy land set in landscaped gardens. Features include coloured waterfalls, haunted dungeons , 'living' fairy tales and nostalgic displays. In addition to the popular Gnomeland , the centre also features the Enchanted Walk, mystical water fountains and Merrygoland, including one of the world's largest tube slides (see page 103)

Webbs of Wychbold
Wychbold, Droitwich, Worcestershire.
Tel: (01527) 861777
Garden centre selling gnomes.

B and A Whelan Ltd
52 High Street, Blue Town, Sheerness, Kent.
Tel: (01795) 663879
The United Kingdom's biggest manufacturers of concrete garden ornaments and statuary. Thousands of gnomes and other figures stand impressively in serried ranks on high shelves in the open air. Follow signs for Sheerness Docks and turn off on Chapel Street.

Gnomes on the Internet

Land of Gnomes
6215 Ferris Square, San Diego, California 92121, USA. Tel: 619-452-0201
Sells the Zeho range of gnomes. Order form on the Internet.

INDEX

ACKNOWLEDGEMENTS

The Automobile Association would like to thank the following libraries, photographers and organisations for their assistance in the preparation of this book.

AKG LONDON 10b, 13b, 26a, 26b, 36a, 36b, 36c, 116b
AMORET TANNER COLLECTION 68d, 68e
R M BALDIN 44b, 93a
BBC WORLDWIDE PUBLISHING 118b
THE BRIDGEMAN ART LIBRARY, LONDON 11b Thor: the Norse god, fishing for the serpent of Midgard, from the boat of the giant Hymir (manuscript) (Royal Library, Copenhagen); 19a 'The Goblins' from 'Peter Pan in Kensington Gardens' by J M Barrie, 1906 by Arthur Rackham (1867–1939); 22b 'The Feast' (early 20th-century illustration); 35b Queen Henrietta Maria and her dwarf Sir Jeffrey Hudson, c1633 by Sir Anthony van Dyck (1599–1641); 110a The Quarrel of Oberon and Titania, 1849 by Sir Joseph Noel Paton (1821–1901); 114c 'The Rhinemaidens teasing Alberich' from 'The Rhinegold and The Valkyrie' by Richard Wagner, 1910 by Arthur Rackham (1867–1939); 116c 'The Wooing of Grunhilde, the mother of Hagen' from 'Siegfried and The Twilight of the Gods' by Richard Wagner, translated by Margaret Armour, 1911 by Arthur Rackham (1867–1939)
BRITSTOCK-IFA LTD 8a
CORBIS UK LTD 112a
SYLVIA CORDAIY PHOTO LIBRARY 20a
DEE CONWAY 110b, 115a
RICHARD DEAN 92
MICHAEL DIGGIN 21a, 23b, 24a, 60b
DAS DEUTSCHE GARTENZWERG MUSEUM 107d,113a, 115a, 122b
MARY EVANS PICTURE LIBRARY 11a, 13a, 15a, 15b, 18a, 20b, 22a, 23d, 28b, 29a, 30a, 30c, 3la, 3lb, 40b, 90, 112c
EFTELING 12a, 27a, 104a, 104b, 105a, 105b
MATTHEW FEARN 119c
GAMMA MAGAZINE 91a, 91b
THE GARDEN PICTURE LIBRARY 2/3, 6a, 6b, 55b
GIRAUDON 24b
THE GNOME RESERVE 34a, 40a, 42, 46c, 61c. 96, 96/7, 97c, 98/9
THE RONALD GRANT ARCHIVE 119a, 119b
ROBERT HARDING PICTURE LIBRARY 39b
HEALTH EDUCATION AUTHORITY 122c
THE KOBAL COLLECTION 118a, 120b
LAMPORT HALL 38b
IRMI LONG 4, 6, 7b, 45a, 55d, 55f, 62a, 64d, 69, 86(1), (2), (3), (4), (5), 87, 87(6), (7), 111a, 124
TERRY MAJOR-BALL 66a
ENA McGINN 49a
'REPRINTED WITH THE KIND PERMISSION OF MILLERS PUBLICATIONS UK, TEL: 01580 76641' 46a/b, 60a, 62b, 63a, 67a, 67b, 114b, 115b, 116a
EDMUND NAGELE FRPS 16b
JENNY NYSTYROM (ELLASON) 16a
ROYAL HORTICULTURE SOCIETY 68a/b/c/f
MAY SCHWARZ 8c
SALISBURY PLAYHOUSE by kind permission 117b
SILVER LYNX 15c, 29b, 49c, 50a, 55c, 56a, 64c
SPECTRUM COLOUR LIBRARY 112b, 113b
HENRY SUTHERLAND 94b, 95a
THAMES TELEVISION 121a
SOUTH HILL PARK ARTS CENTRE, BRACKNELL by kind permission 117a
YORK ARCHAELOGICAL TRUST 32b

All the remaining pictures are held in the Asssociation's own library (AA Photo Library), with contributions from:
M BIRKITT 38a, 39a, 94a
PAUL KENWARD 27b
ALEX KOUPRIANOF 52, 58/9 65b, 106a, 106b, 106c, 106d, 107a, 107b, 107c, 107e, 108a, 108b, 108c, 108d, 108e
ROGER MOSS 17b, 28a, 33, 36d, 37a, 37b, 41a, 41b, 44a, 47b, 51b, 53, 59, 61a, 63c, 63d, 63f, 64a,64b,89, 97a, 97b, 98a, 98b, 98c, 99a, 99b, 100a, 100b, 100/l, 101a,101b, 101c, 102a, 102b, 102c, 102d, 103a, 103b, 103c, 103d, 109, 124
CLIVE SAWYER 35a
RICK STRANGE 56b
WYN VOYSEY 7a, 46d, 49b, 92b, 93b, 93c, 93d

Illustrations by ALAN ROE